# COOKIN' IT
## WITH KIX

# COOKIN' IT WITH KIX

## THE ART OF CELEBRATING AND THE FUN OF OUTDOOR COOKING

## KIX BROOKS

W PUBLISHING GROUP

AN IMPRINT OF THOMAS NELSON

Published in Nashville, Tennessee, by W Publishing Group, an imprint of Thomas Nelson. W Publishing and Thomas Nelson are registered trademarks of HarperCollins Christian Publishing, Inc.

Photography by Tambi Lane Photography at Tambilane.com

Food and Prop Styling by Caitlin Kelly, Tambi Lane, and Donna Britt

Pastel Azteca recipe is reprinted courtesy of the authors of the book *Enchiladas Aztec to Tex-Mex* by Chris Waters Dunn and Cappy Lawton, published by Trinity University Press.

Thomas Nelson, Inc., titles may be purchased in bulk for educational, business, fund-raising, or sales promotional use. For information, please e-mail SpecialMarkets@ThomasNelson.com.

**Library of Congress Cataloging-in-Publication Data is on file**
**with the publisher and the Library of Congress.**

ISBN 978-0-7180-8486-8

*Printed in the United States of America*
16 17 18 19 20 RRD 6 5 4 3 2 1

I'd like to dedicate this cookbook to all the folks out there who have been so intimidated by the thought of cooking that they have missed the joy of finding the right stuff, preparing, and serving it up themselves. I hope this book inspires you to fire up the grill or stove or skillet or something and make a mess. Good luck! You'll figure it out!

# CONTENTS

# INTRODUCTION

*L*ast year, as I wrapped up filming on the Cooking Channel program *Steak Out with Kix Brooks*, I realized I had discovered a whole new appreciation for cooking, enjoying great food, and the importance of pairing food and drinks, wine in particular. I already knew that food and cooking have so much more to offer than just keeping you from being hungry. Where I grew up, hunting and fishing and even taking a drive to find something fresh, whether it was fresh oysters or shrimp in South Louisiana or fresh summertime peaches in North Louisiana, were all part of the process. Going after something "special" to eat was always accompanied by a great adventure and made for a good story. Those stories make the food taste that much better when it hits the table or tailgate.

This book is as much about the "experience" of eating as it is about cooking. I don't claim to be a chef, and if you bought this book, chances are you're not a chef either, but we don't have to be. The part of the world and the family that I came from taught me this: cooking is something you take pride in and have fun doing. Preparing food isn't meant just for the "women folk" down South either; the ladies can sure get it done, but there's a prideful competition between men and women about who does what the best, and there's a lot of teamwork as well.

At a fairly young age, I learned to fry fish and potatoes (and just about everything else) and how to grill a steak. I also was taught how to deal with venison and all the other game and fish we hunted and caught. Wild game is a world unto itself, and I'll share some tips from some great outdoor cooks along with recipes and tricks from friends and family.

I can't tell you how many times before concerts I have gone out into the parking lots to hang with the fans and just been blown away by the stuff they had going on their grills and the platters of great-looking snacks on their tailgates. Tailgating is an art form, and whether it's a football game or a Kenny Chesney festival, knowing your way around parking-lot parties is important. I'm here to help you out.

To complete the whole package, we mustn't forget the beverages. The drinks can be as simple as making fresh margaritas to go with Mexican food or knowing what wines to pair with a chocolate dessert. I will do my best to give some basics on what I think works well.

Finally, I'm looking forward to reliving some of the memories I had growing up: making fig and peach preserves with my grandparents and taking turns with my cousins turning the crank on a homemade ice cream churn, catching fish on the lake where I lived with my dad, and showing up with dinner where the grease was always hot and ready. We had a big country kitchen outside next to the house, and there was no end to what might be steaming or boiling or frying or smoking. Cooking was just part of living, and the living was good.

I hope the stories will be fun and the tips will be helpful as a quick reference for food that is delicious and easy to prepare, all contributing to a lifestyle that you can share with your friends and family that's sure to come with a full stomach and many great memories of your own.

ENJOY!
KIX BROOKS

# CHAPTER 1
# WHERE I COME FROM

# LOUISIANA ROOTS

*H*ello! I'm Kix Brooks, and yes, I'm the Brooks part of the country music duo Brooks & Dunn. I'm also the host of the nationally syndicated radio show *American Country Countdown*, the former host of *Steak Out with Kix Brooks* on the Cooking Channel, and a founding owner/partner of Arrington Vineyards outside of Nashville,

Tennessee. I've lived in Tennessee for years now, but I was born and raised in Louisiana, and my family roots run deep there.

It's hard to describe what being from Louisiana means. Every state has an identity and its own culture, but I'm not sure any is more recognizable or more diverse than Louisiana's. Louisiana is known as the "Sportsman's Paradise," which suits us well, but who doesn't think about food and cooking when they think about Louisiana, especially New Orleans.

This might be a good time to explain the difference between Creole and Cajun cooking, as I understand it. Creole cooking is more prominent in the southern part of the state, and it especially shines through in the great restaurants of New Orleans, where this elegant treatment of classic Louisiana cooking becomes an art form in itself. I think most chefs would tell you that Cajun cooking comes from the more casual side of things, no less appetizing, but more from the backyard or boat dock, home kitchen, or duck camp. This book is my own hybrid collection of dishes inspired by the food of my homeland and actual family recipes. It's Cajun, it's Creole, it's Tex-Mex, it's Southern, and it's even Northern since my wife is from Massachusetts. There are some generations-old, hand-me-down dishes as well as some brand-new ideas that seem to fit right in there with the flavors I love.

I've certainly never claimed to be a chef or honestly even attempted to recreate most of the great meals I've had at fine New Orleans establishments like Commander's Palace or Antoine's. But meals I've had at those places have been inspiring, and once you get a taste, like most good things, you can't wait to do it again. And then on a good night I'm thinking, *How hard can Bananas Foster be anyway? Let's catch something on fire!*

I moved to Tennessee straight from New Orleans where I played at Tipitina's bar and the Old Absinthe House on Bourbon Street. My last run there was seventy-two nights in a row, and the culture, the food, and the all-around vibe are proudly tattooed on my soul forever. The older I get, the more the memories and the stories continue to simmer in my brain like a good gumbo. So, if something I say in here isn't exactly true, it's not because that's not how I remember it.

Throughout this cookbook I will be telling stories about growing up in Louisiana as well as telling tales about my adventures since that precious time of my youth. My stories will certainly include other people, namely my closest family members and my dearest friends. I'll be introducing you to those folks along the way. I'll tell you right now that it was my grandfather on my mother's side, Mr. Kleber Samuel Thompson, known as D-Daddy to his family, and my father, Leon Eric Brooks Jr., who taught me the most about cooking and appreciating food.

My dad and D-Daddy taught me how to do the things that all young boys in the South were expected to have some know-how about: how to catch and fry fish, how to grill up a steak, how to shuck oysters.

The most important thing that I learned from my father and grandfather, though, was that, no matter what your walk of life, the outdoors and sharing that outdoor time with your family was where life "found its own way." Adventure lives outdoors; nature is unpredictable, so of course, great stories are born there. For example, fishing isn't just about catching fish—a lot of things happen between loading that boat and sitting down at the dinner table. That's the inspiration behind this book.

# BEEFMASTER

*M*ike Leatherwood has been driving me around in a tour bus for more than twenty years; we've literally been millions of miles together. Mike lives on my farm now, and most of the time when he's not driving or riding a tractor, he is watching the RFD channel to check on the price of cattle, new cattle breeds, and breeding techniques.

But let me start at the beginning: One night we were driving along, and I asked Mike if he could have any kind of cattle, what kind would he want to own? He quickly responded that Beefmaster would be his breed of choice, so I said, "Well, let's get some!"

There began what has become a story of learning, hard work, trips around the country, supporting young people showing cattle, and most importantly raising high-end beef cattle.

There *is* a difference in the quality of meat you buy in the store and the beef that you get in a fine restaurant. Many times great restaurants have their own herds, but at the very least they are sourcing Prime beef. Generally speaking, USDA Choice beef is in your supermarket, and it's not bad, but it's not the same thing as USDA Prime. Bottom line is to always get the highest quality meat you can get, and your food will taste so much better.

There are cows that come from the giant stockyards, and then there are cattle that are raised on farms where they're taken care of and fed to make the best product before they're delivered to market. That's what Mike and I are doing raising Beefmaster cattle—trying to get the best product we can to take to market.

Being a proponent of farm-raised produce, I've also supported and admired families who encourage their children to get involved in 4-H and other agriculture programs that teach them about responsibility and what goes in to raising animals as well as the other foods that wind up on the dinner table.

I can remember looking through a tall pipe fence in Fort Worth, Texas, a couple of years ago, watching a group of young people show cattle. There was a cute little blonde-headed girl who wasn't half as tall as the big heifer she was leading around the ring; I had noticed her on a stool earlier in the day with soap and a hose washing this big cow, but I never dreamed she would actually be showing it. Anyway, it was touch and go in the ring now as to who was leading whom, but she had her jaw cocked, and she was making her way with a focused determination. I couldn't help but start pulling for her. There were probably twelve other young people in there with fine-looking animals, all doing their best, and I thought, *What a great program.*

It made me proud to realize how much good comes from this industry that people are not aware of. When they all lined up and the judges made their choice, my little blonde buddy won the blue ribbon. She was cool too; she didn't jump up and down and make the other contestants feel bad, but she smiled from ear to ear and gave her big heifer a hug. I felt my eyes well up at the thought of what it all meant. Later on she saw me and asked for an autograph, and I said, "Are you kidding me? You're the rock star here!" I still have her autograph on my sale program from that amazing day.

Raising cattle is yet another connection I have to this food thing, and I have several steak recipes to share if you'll just hang with me.

# ARRINGTON VINEYARDS

I've always liked wine. I was like every other Romeo in college; it seemed like a great way to act sophisticated when you had a date who seemed a little out of your league or

when you just wanted to do something a little more special than a beer in a bar. I didn't really know much other than I liked it and that Mateus made a good candleholder.

As time went on, like most things that you take an interest in, I started to learn there was a lot more to this wine world than I had realized. I attended some nice dinners that had wine that tasted different from the wine I was used to. I had different wines with different foods during the same meal, and, wow, things were getting fun. Before I knew it, I was really paying attention to taste and to labels and, of course, to price tags.

But the truth is, you don't have to spend a fortune to learn about nice wines from all over the world, and the more I learned, the more I wanted to share my knowledge. Eventually I met some friends with the same passion for this wine thing, and we decided to create a world of our own right where we lived in Nashville where people could come and listen to music, enjoy a great view of the Harpeth Valley, and taste as many as eighteen different varieties of wine. It was one of the craziest leaps of faith I've ever taken, but we starting planting vines way back in 2002, and in 2007, after a lot of hard work, Arrington Vineyards was born. Thanks to the support of thousands of wine lovers from around the country, we are still going strong. My partner and winemaker Kip Summers helps me out throughout this book, offering you a few good wine-food pairing ideas.

# COWRITER DONNA BRITT

*I*'ve been hosting *American Country Countdown* since 2006, and it was quite a learning process. I probably wouldn't have survived if the radio network hadn't had the good sense to bring in a great producer and writer. Her name is Donna Britt, and our friendship was almost immediate. Some people, you just know right away, are the kind of friends you want to take care of and keep forever. Donna didn't just know what she was doing, she was a good listener, and for people like me who love to hear themselves talk, that is very important.

If you're a "talker," you can learn a lot from a good listener, because if you are really given all the time you need to hear yourself, eventually you might actually figure out when to stop talking, and ultimately you might figure out the things that you don't really even need to say. Then, God forbid, you might start to pay attention to what someone else has to offer. Like my dad used to say, "Your transmitter works really good. You might want to try your receiver out some time!" Of course, I was too busy talking at the time to understand what he meant.

Thankfully as I got older and met interesting people like Donna, I did start to listen a little more, and I learned that Donna was really into cooking. She even hosted a local TV show about cooking. My engineer in the studio, Lonnie Napier, also liked to cook. All that led to many fun discussions about how cooking works in different parts of the country. We found a common bond that was outside of just trying to make a good radio show. When I decided to share more about the culture I came from and the food that went with it, Donna was the obvious choice to help me put it all together.

I knew she could help make my long-winded descriptions easy to understand. I also knew she would cook everything that would be written about in this book, so you can be assured this stuff actually works. I'm hoping, too, that some of the fun and heartfelt joy that we both experienced putting this book together will live on in the pages ahead. That's the point here: we *ain't* in surgery; this is supposed to be fun. You might burn something or realize it could use more of this or that, but have some fun doing it and remember eating it is the easy part.

You would expect me to say that I could never have done this without Donna, but the truth is I don't think I could have done this with anyone else. I'll be forever grateful to her for staying after me and making this happen.

# FOOD IS A CELEBRATION!

*W*hen we think of New Year's and food, we think of red beans and rice or black-eyed peas; Valentine's Day is chocolate; Thanksgiving is turkey, and so on and so on for the civilized world, but where I come from, *every* day is based around a food party. We're not just cooking to eat; we're getting together to cook, and then we'll eat.

What are we having and where did it come from and how fresh is it are all part of the conversation and the fun food culture, which is not the same as what I consider being a foodie. It's not about some interesting lil' thing on your plate that you have to guess what it is and try and imagine the twenty amazing spices and flavors that are coming out of it; I've done that, and it's fascinating, and pairing those flavors with some amazing wine that complements them is a game in itself.

That's not what this book is about though; this book is about rolling up your sleeves, not worrying too much about anything except who you want to share the fun with, and if a recipe doesn't work like you want it to the first time you try it, you have a drink and try it again. If you don't like the way *that* wine tastes with your whatever, try this *other* wine. The fun is in the hang, smoking up the grill or the kitchen, and working your way to becoming a good cook. As far as that wine is concerned, I will give you some suggestions I don't think you'll mind trying.

The deal is, food doesn't have to be expensive, and it's not hard to cook it yourself. What you can do at home is a level of good times, storytelling, and a filling-up-the-plate experience you're just not going to get at a restaurant. You can do this! You might want to start with chapter 8, Libations, Cocktails, and Beverages; regardless, let's go.

# CHAPTER 2
# COOK OUT!

(favorite recipes for fish fries, grilling
out, and other big gatherings)

# COUNTRY KITCHEN

*N*o son ever loved a father more than I loved my old man. There's not enough room in this book to tell that whole story; it would take a lifetime. But I do have time to tell you that some of the best fun he and I ever shared was at our camp on Lake Bistineau outside of Shreveport, Louisiana.

That's where we had the original outdoor kitchen, which we called the Country Kitchen, and where I first learned how to set things on fire—I mean, cook!

The Country Kitchen was a concrete slab, probably twenty by thirty feet, with a roof over it. On that slab were half a dozen rocking chairs, a few tables for drinks and ashtrays, and a big square brick enclosure, about three feet high, maybe five feet long and four feet wide. Inside the enclosure was a grill with two holes cut in it for two large gas burners. This was our fish and tater cooker, turkey fryer, and, most importantly, our shrimp boiler (we'll get the shrimp boiling in chapter 4).

If you like to cook at all, make sure you can cook outside because that's what it's all about. With a simple roof to keep the sun and rain off and some kind of fire, you're good to go. I'm convinced that every house needs a good gas cooker, and I'm not talking about the grill where you cook steaks. I'm talking about a setup where you can have a big pot of hot oil or boiling water, because even if you're just boiling potatoes, it's more fun to cook in the great outdoors. I swear it tastes better.

Where I come from, folks do a lot of cooking and barbecuing and picnicking and tailgating outside. Honestly, I think that's why so many "wild" foods are so popular in Louisiana. Obviously, the seafood and wild game can be caught or bagged fresh, but even if you get it at the grocery store, cooking it outside is a great social activity. All that fresh air is good for you, too, despite how much grease you may be using to fry up your catch.

# WINE NOTES

*I*n this chapter we have everything from fried fish and raw oysters to big pots of jambalaya and etouffée to thick rib eye steaks. I warned you that I was going to give you some wine tips, and for me, the most fun way to do that is to tell a story. So here we go!

Not too long ago a group of friends and I were in New Orleans for a Tennessee Titans football game. We had the opportunity to have a meal at one of America's most outstanding restaurants, Galatoire's, a century-old fine-dining establishment on Bourbon Street. That evening's meal covered a lot of territory, so I thought it would make

sense to take you through the wine to give you a real-life example of what to drink with what.

We first opened a nice, dry Burgundy, and it paired well with multiple courses that we knew were on the way: oysters, crab salad, and fish. Burgundies are made in the Burgundy region of eastern France. They are typically dry red wines made from pinot noir grapes and white wines made from chardonnay grapes. Of course we were taking full advantage of French Quarter cooking, and since we hadn't had enough to eat yet, we finished the meal with an unbelievable filet mignon with a nice Bearnaise sauce. Red meat screams for red wine, and I tend to lean toward chewy cabs (cabernet sauvignons) or merlots.

Of course we could have gone a slightly different direction at Galatoire's. I like the idea of sparkling wine or brut champagne with oysters. If oysters are served as an appetizer, sparkling wine and champagne are both great palate cleansers. Another great starter, foie gras, also goes well with champagne. Speaking of foie gras, if you're lucky enough to have access to this goose liver prepared the proper way, try it with a French sauterne, made from semillon, sauvignon blanc, and muscadelle grapes.

If you want to keep things a bit simpler, it's fun to find a good white wine that plays in the middle, meaning it will go down nicely with everything from oysters and crab to goose liver.

The president of Arrington Vineyards is Kip Summers. Kip and I have been

partners since the beginning of the vineyard when he was the original winemaker. He still oversees the winemaking. Since Arrington has been winning wine awards since we opened, I always defer to Kip for pairing suggestions and here's what Kip has to say about what to drink with oysters:

"For oysters, my first choice would be a crisp, dry sauvignon blanc from New Zealand or Sancerre, France. I've heard that classic French chablis works well, though I've never tried that combo. It would have to be an acidic low- or no-oak–style chablis to match with the oysters. California chardonnay is typically too oaky and lacking in acidity to pair well with oysters. I also think a dry, acidic pale rosé would work, too, and the Spanish white wine called Albariño would be great. What all of these suggestions have in common is a lemony acidity that pairs well with the oysters."

# D-DADDY'S FRIED FISH

*KIX STORY*: My grandpa, Kleber Thompson, known as D-Daddy to the grandkids, was a small-town businessman and the mayor of Marion, Louisiana. He owned the general store there and was also the president of the local bank. He'd spend the day going about his business while constantly quizzing his customers and all the locals about where the fish were biting. When he'd get off work, he'd grab me and his Jon boat and throw the boat in the back of his pickup truck, and off we'd go to whatever fishing hole was hot that day. We'd fish with crickets or worms or sometimes even catalpa worms, which we'd find in nearby catalpa trees. Cool thing about all that, D-Daddy and I would end up at the dinner table with the family, eating what we'd caught. I should mention that it was D-Daddy who fried up the fish. My Memaw loved me like nobody's business, but she couldn't cook anything!

*Here's my favorite recipe for frying fish. It'll taste better if you grab your favorite kid and go catch 'em yourself. Of course, if you don't live near a fishing hole or if it's not fishing season, you can substitute store-bought fish. Fresh or frozen cod is a good choice. The amounts below will work for several small fish. If you need to fry more, just increase the amounts—double, triple, or quadruple if you need to.*

*The seasonings listed below are just a general idea of how you can spice up the cornmeal. Don't be afraid to experiment with spices and see what you like. Think of it this way: you can dip anything in milk and make something stick to it. So take advantage of the hot oil and play. Dip that fish in milk, drag it through the spiced-up cornmeal, and go for it!*

**Peanut oil, for frying, enough to fill your big pot at least halfway to the top**

**1 cup cornmeal, white or yellow**

**½ teaspoon salt, plus more for sprinkling on fried fish**

**½ teaspoon black pepper, plus more for sprinkling on fried fish**

½ teaspoon garlic powder

½ teaspoon onion powder

⅛ teaspoon cayenne pepper

Freshly caught fish (I grew up eating bream and sun perch), cleaned and cooked whole

½ cup milk

Lemon juice

Lemon wedges, for serving

Tartar sauce, for serving

Fill a heavy pot at least halfway full of oil, and set it over medium heat. (That's medium heat, not high heat; we're not trying to burn the house down.) Test the oil every few minutes until it gets up to temperature. You can throw a pinch of cornmeal in the oil, and when it bubbles and immediately starts to turn brown, it's ready. Or you could use a deep-fry or candy thermometer to make sure the temperature is between 350 and 375 degrees. Or you could get real dangerous and try my dad's great "match trick" (see Kix Tip below).

Mix the cornmeal, salt, pepper, garlic powder, onion powder, and cayenne together in a small bowl.

Dip the fish pieces into the milk, then drag them through the cornmeal mixture. (If you like, you can plop the fish into the cornmeal and gently roll it around to get it coated.)

Drop the coated fish into the hot oil, a few at a time to avoid crowding the pot and bringing the temperature of the oil down. Fry until golden brown. When the fish floats, it's done, but if you want it browner, let it go a little longer—just be careful not to burn it. Drain the fish pieces on a paper towel-lined platter, or just toss the cooked fish onto a piece of butcher paper or a cut-up brown paper grocery sack. Sprinkle the fish with a pinch of salt and pepper and lemon juice right after you remove it from the hot oil.

Serve the fish with lemon wedges and tartar sauce, or just pick up a warm chunk and eat it plain; you won't be sorry.

*KIX TIP*: To turn your fish fry into a full-blown party, go ahead and fry up some Classic Fried Fries and Hushpuppies with Green Onions to go with your fish, and invite your friends and neighbors over for the feast. This Old-Fashioned Fish Fry is a good spread for an *any* day get-together.

*KIX TIP*: People ask all the time, "How do you know when your grease or oil is hot enough to fry?" The short answer is somewhere between 300 and 375 degrees. But you could also use my dad's great match trick. While he and I were jawing away, waiting for the oil to get hot, we would drop a large kitchen match, one with a white tip, right into the oil. When it was hot enough, the match would light itself, and that's when we would add whatever we were cooking to the hot pot of frying oil. I'm not kidding. It actually works!

# CLASSIC FRIED FRIES

*KIX STORY*: My dad had a boathouse on Lake Bistineau not far from my hometown of Shreveport. It was there that I learned how to catch, clean, and eat perch and bream (also known as bluegill). I'm not kidding you when I say my hands are still sore from cleaning fish.

**2 pounds potatoes, russets, or red or Yukon Golds (4 to 5 potatoes)**
**Ice water**
**2 quarts canola or peanut oil**

**1 tablespoon sea salt**
**1 teaspoon black pepper**

Wash the potatoes, and cut into slices. You can peel them if you want, but there's no need. Place the slices in a large bowl of ice water, and let soak for 15 to 30 minutes. Heat the oil in a heavy pot to 325 degrees. A deep-fry thermometer is very helpful.

Remove the potatoes from the water, and pat them dry with paper towels. Add a couple handfuls of potatoes to the hot oil and cook until light brown in color, 5 to 7 minutes. Remove the potatoes from the oil and drain them on a rack or on paper towels. Continue until all potatoes are fried.

Raise the temperature of the oil to 350 degrees.

Fry the potatoes again, dropping two handfuls at a time into the hot oil, until golden brown, about 2 minutes. Remove from the oil, shake off the excess oil, and put into a big bowl or platter. Sprinkle the salt and pepper on the potatoes.

❯ **Makes 8 servings.**

 **Everything's good deep-fried!**

# HUSHPUPPIES WITH GREEN ONIONS

Up to 2 cups cornmeal, yellow or white

Scant ¼ cup all-purpose flour (optional)

2 teaspoons salt

1 teaspoon baking powder

½ teaspoon baking soda

¾ cup buttermilk

1 egg, beaten

Dash of hot sauce (optional)

Several green onions, chopped

2 tablespoons bacon drippings or canola oil

Mix the cornmeal, flour (if using), salt, baking powder, and baking soda in a large bowl. Add the buttermilk and beaten egg, and stir until well mixed. Stir in the hot sauce, onion, and bacon drippings. (If you want a cornmeal-only hushpuppy, leave out the flour, and after you add the milk and egg, add more cornmeal if the batter is too thin to form into soft balls.)

You can fry these in the same oil you used for the fish and fries if you want; otherwise pour the oil in a large, heavy pot halfway full and heat it to 350 to 360 degrees.

Roll about a tablespoon of batter into a soft ball, and gently drop or slide it into the hot oil. You can use a slotted spoon to lower the balls into the oil if you want. Fry until the hushpuppies are golden brown and rise to the surface, 2 to 3 minutes. Drain on paper towels. Serve immediately.

❯ **Makes 18 to 20.**

*KIX TIP:* You can add anything you want to this basic hushpuppy batter. Maybe throw in a few ounces of Cheddar cheese or a fresh, chopped jalapeño pepper, or both. You've got hot oil, so have some fun with it and experiment.

# BARBECUE SHRIMP IN THE SHELL

*KIX STORY:* Fishing for shrimp is something you typically do in late spring off the Louisiana coast, and it's something I've done my share of over the years. Gulf shrimp are still my favorite shrimp to eat, and I love the simplicity of tossing a few in a pan with some butter or into a vat of boiling water and eating them as soon as they're done, which is in just a few minutes. I usually recommend leaving shrimp in their shells when you're grilling or sautéing them because the shell holds in flavor. In this recipe you use the shells separately to create a flavorful barbecue sauce. Just remember: shells = flavor!

While this recipe has a lot of ingredients, it's simple to make. Just prep everything before you start, and you'll be licking the plate in no time.

*The warm waters off the Gulf Coast of the United States are home to several species of shrimp. Depending on the species, shrimp can range from 1 to 10 inches in size and display a wide range of colors and patterns. For this riff on the now popular shrimp-and-grits dish you'll find on restaurant menus throughout the South, we're turning the grits into a waffle. Of course you could also make a pot of creamy, cheesy grits to serve with the Barbecue Shrimp or keep things simple and toss out a loaf of crusty bread to sop up the sauce.*

**3 pounds large shrimp, in the shell**
**2 tablespoons KB's Shreveport Shake Seasoning (see recipe in chapter 6) or any Creole or Cajun seasoning**
**Freshly ground black pepper**
**2 tablespoons olive oil, divided**
**1/4 cup chopped onion**
**2 tablespoons minced garlic**
**3 bay leaves**
**3 lemons, cut into quarters**
**2 cups water**
**1/2 cup Worcestershire sauce**

**1/4 cup dry white wine**
**1/4 teaspoon salt**
**1/4 teaspoon black pepper**
**1/4 teaspoon smoked paprika**
**1/4 teaspoon chipotle powder**
**1 cup heavy cream**
**1 tablespoon dried oregano, crumbled**
**2 teaspoons Worcestershire sauce**
**2 tablespoons unsalted butter**
**1 tablespoon chopped chives, for garnish**
**Corn Grit Waffles (see recipe)**

Peel the shrimp, leaving their tails attached. Reserve the shells. Sprinkle the shrimp with half of the seasoning and black pepper. Make sure the shrimp is well coated with the seasoning. Refrigerate the shrimp.

Heat 1 tablespoon of the olive oil in a large pot over high heat. When the oil is hot, add the onion and garlic, and sauté for 1 minute. Add the shrimp shells, remaining seasoning, bay leaves, lemons, water, Worcestershire sauce, wine, salt, pepper, paprika, and chipotle powder. Stir well, and bring to a boil.

Reduce the heat to low, and simmer for 30 minutes. Remove from the heat, and let cool for about 15 minutes; then strain, reserving the liquid.

Place the liquid back in the pot, and bring to a boil over high heat. Cook the sauce until thick and darker in color, about 15 minutes.

Heat the remaining 1 tablespoon of olive oil in a large skillet over high heat. When the oil is hot, add the shrimp, and sauté for a few minutes, occasionally shaking the skillet. Add the cream and the sauce, stir, and simmer for 3 minutes. Remove the shrimp with a slotted spoon, and mound it on a warm platter.

Stir the oregano and Worcestershire sauce into the sauce. Whisk the butter into the sauce. Remove from the heat and spoon over the shrimp and around the platter. Garnish with chives and serve with Corn Grit Waffles.

❯ **Makes 6 to 8 servings.**

# CORN GRIT WAFFLES

*These are unsweetened waffles with a nice bite. If you bake them longer than usual in the waffle iron, until the outsides are a bit crunchy, they will stand up well to the barbecue sauce. If you prefer a sweeter taste, just add a teaspoon or two of sugar to the dry ingredients.*

**1/2 cup water**
**3/4 teaspoon salt, divided**
**1 cup polenta or grits**
**4 tablespoons unsalted butter**
**1 cup milk**

**1 cup all-purpose flour**
**1/2 tablespoon baking powder**
**1/2 teaspoon baking soda**
**Oil, for greasing waffle iron**

Bring the water and 1/4 teaspoon of the salt to a boil. Stir in the polenta. Reduce the heat to low, and stir in the butter and milk. Mix well.

Whisk the flour, baking powder, baking soda, and the remaining 1/2 teaspoon of salt together in a large bowl.

Stir the polenta into the flour mixture. Mix well. Set aside to rest for 5 minutes while the waffle iron heats.

Preheat the waffle iron and brush lightly with oil. Spoon or ladle the batter onto waffle iron, and cook until browned and crunchy. Remove the waffles from the iron and place on a baking rack to cool; do not stack. (If you prefer, you can keep them warm in a 220-degree oven.)

Cut the waffles into quarters, and place a piece on each serving plate, spooning the Barbecue Shrimp and its sauce on top.

❷ **Makes 4 to 6.**

*KIX TIP:* Both polenta, associated with Italy, and grits, associated with the American South, are made from stone-ground cornmeal. Most grits are made from a class of corn called dent corn, while most polenta is made from a class of corn called flint corn. Grits can come across as mushy, while polenta is often more coarse. To keep it simple, you can get yourself a bag of "coarse cornmeal" at the grocery store, and use that in any recipe that calls for polenta or grits.

*KIX TIP:* You can use whole milk, 2 percent milk, or skim milk for these waffles. If the batter seems too thick, add a bit more milk.

# AUNT GRACE'S CRAWFISH ETOUFFÉE

**KIX STORY:** One of the great heartaches of my life is that I'm allergic to crawfish. Yeah, it's the only thing I'm allergic to, and it really bums me out because Aunt Grace's Crawfish Etouffée is the best. I know because the two times I tried it, it tasted delicious. I'm not saying anything is worth swelling up and getting sick over, but if anything was, it would be her etouffée. And yes, I'm that stubborn; I wasn't willing to accept I was allergic the first time around, so, of course, I had to try it a second time.

*In Southern Louisiana, etouffée is a cooking technique that means to smother or cook something in its own juices. If you start your etouffée with a roux (see Getcha Some Duck Gumbo in chapter 3 for a basic roux recipe) like this recipe suggests, you essentially have a stew, which is then served over rice. If you're not from Louisiana or you haven't been to culinary school, you might be a bit confused as to how etouffée is different from jambalaya or gumbo. Here's a quick rundown of all three:*

*Etouffée is a stew, usually containing crawfish or seafood, which is served over rice.*

*Jambalaya has rice cooked into the dish and has no roux.*

*Gumbo is roux-based and served over rice. It often has okra in it.*

1 pound Louisiana crawfish tails, thawed, or shrimp, tails removed

2 tablespoons canola oil

2 tablespoons butter

4 tablespoons all-purpose flour

1 large onion, diced

1 green bell pepper, diced

2 celery ribs, diced

4 cloves garlic, minced

1 ½ cups water

1 teaspoon salt, or to taste

¼ teaspoon white pepper, or to taste

¼ teaspoon garlic powder, or to taste

¼ teaspoon cayenne pepper, or to taste

3 to 4 green onions, chopped

Basic Rice (see recipe)

Handful of parsley, chopped, for garnish

Crusty bread, for serving

Thaw the crawfish tails, and let them hang in fridge until you're ready for them. Do not prewash.

In a heavy, preferably cast-iron, skillet, heat the oil over medium-low heat. When hot, add the butter. Let the butter melt, then stir into the oil. Add the flour, and cook, stirring constantly to avoid burning. After a few minutes, it should become a nice tan color. You're making a roux here.

Add the onion, bell pepper, and celery to the roux. Sauté until the onions are translucent, for about 5 to 10 minutes. Add the garlic, stir, and cook for another minute.

Place the water in a large bowl and add the crawfish. Stir them around to release their juices.

**KIX TIP**: If you're not in or around Louisiana, you probably won't be able to find crawfish tails at the grocery store, so feel free to replace the crawfish with shrimp.

Once veggies are cooked down a bit, add the crawfish juice and water to the pan. Increase the heat to medium-high, and bring to a boil. Add the salt, white pepper, garlic powder, and cayenne. Taste to see if you want to adjust the seasonings, and add more of anything you like.

Reduce the heat to low, and simmer for 20 minutes. If the sauce gets too thick, add a little water. After 20 minutes, add the crawfish tails and green onions, and cook for another 5 minutes.

Serve over rice, and garnish with parsley. Serve with crusty bread.

❯ **Makes 8–10 servings.**

# BASIC RICE

**1 cup rice, brown, white, wild, long-grain, short-grain, or your favorite**

**2 cups water**

**1 tablespoon butter or olive oil**

**1 teaspoon salt**

Stir the rice into the water in a 2-quart saucepan. Bring to a boil over medium-high heat, then reduce the heat to low. Simmer, covered, until all the water is absorbed, typically 20 to 45 minutes, depending on type of rice, type of pot used, etc. Leave a tiny opening or vent between the lid and the pot while the rice is simmering. Don't be afraid to peek in to see how your rice is doing.

**KIX TIP**: People go on and on about how you need to put the lid on tightly when you're cooking rice and how you shouldn't remove the lid to check the rice while it's simmering. Well, I'm telling you the opposite: don't put the lid on tightly and peek in every 10 minutes or so. I think the real key is to hold off on stirring in the salt and any other spices until after the rice is cooked and the water is completely absorbed.

Once the water is completely absorbed, remove from the heat. Stir in the butter and salt and any other spices you like, cover, and let the rice sit for 10 minutes. Fluff with fork before serving.

❯ **Makes 4 servings.**

# BIG OL' MESS JAMBALAYA

*Jambalaya is a classic Creole dish. Its roots are French and Spanish (think paella), and it's different from a gumbo in that it is not roux-based. Also, the rice is cooked in this dish. Think about packing this pot of goodness into a cooler without any ice, so it stays nice and hot, and taking it to your next tailgate party or picnic or maybe even a Mardi Gras parade.*

1 large chicken or duck, 4–6 pounds, cut up

3 tablespoons KB's Shreveport Shake Seasoning (see recipe in chapter 6) or other Cajun or Creole seasoning, divided

2 tablespoons vegetable oil

1 pound andouille or other spicy smoked sausage, cut into 1/4-inch pieces

2 cups chopped onions, yellow or white

1 cup chopped green or red bell pepper

1/2 cup chopped celery

1 teaspoon salt

1/2 teaspoon cayenne pepper

1/2 teaspoon freshly ground black pepper

2 cups peeled, seeded, and chopped tomatoes (optional)

1 tablespoon chopped garlic

3 bay leaves

2 cups long-grain rice, white or brown

2 teaspoons minced fresh thyme

2 quarts chicken broth

1 pound medium shrimp, peeled and deveined

1 cup chopped green onions

1/2 cup minced flat-leaf parsley

Season the chicken with 2 tablespoons of the seasoning. Heat the vegetable oil in a large, heavy pot over medium-high heat. Add the chicken, skin side down, and sear for 5 minutes. Turn and sear on the other side for 3 minutes. Remove the chicken from the pot, and drain on paper towels.

Add the sausage to the pot, and cook, stirring, until browned. Add the "Holy Trinity" of onions, bell peppers, and celery along with the salt, cayenne, and black pepper. Cook, stirring often, until the veggies are softened, about 5 minutes. Add the tomatoes, garlic, and bay leaves, and cook, stirring, until the tomatoes release some juice, about 2 minutes. Add the rice, and cook, stirring, for 2 minutes.

Add the thyme, broth, and chicken. Bring to a boil.

*KIX TIP:* You could leave the tomatoes out of this jambalaya. Classic Creole recipes usually call for tomatoes, while southern or rural Creole recipes do not. It's really up to you and your taste buds. I like it either way.

Reduce the heat to medium-low, cover, and simmer, stirring occasionally, until the rice is done, about 30 minutes.

Season the shrimp with the remaining 1 tablespoon of seasoning. Add the shrimp to the pot, and cook until they turn pink, about 5 minutes. Remove the pot from heat. Let sit, covered, for at least 15 minutes.

Add the green onions and parsley to the pot and stir gently. Remove the bay leaves. Taste the jambalaya, and add more salt, pepper, or cayenne if needed. Serve directly from pot.

❯ **Makes 8 to 10 servings.**

# GRILLED OYSTERS

*No matter what time of the year it is, we're always fishing for something down where I come from. In November and December, it's red fish and oysters. There's nothing better than fresh oysters on the half shell, and there are a million ways to fix 'em up for good eating, but here are a couple spins I highly recommend.*

**Fresh oysters, as many as you want**

**Lemon-Garlic Butter (see recipe)**

**Lemon wedges**

**Hot sauce**

**Chopped parsley, chives, or other fresh herbs (optional)**

Heat the grill to medium-high. Scrub the oysters with a stiff brush or scouring pad under running water. Place, cupped side down, on the grill grate. Cover the grill, and cook until the oysters begin to open, about 2 minutes. Transfer the oysters to a platter. Throw away any oysters that don't open.

Let cool slightly; then use an oyster knife or screwdriver to pry the shells open, keeping the cupped side down and retaining as much liquid as possible. Cut the muscles connecting the oysters to their shells with a paring knife or oyster knife.

Serve warm with Lemon-Garlic Butter, lemon wedges, and hot sauce. Sprinkle fresh chopped herbs on top if desired.

# LEMON-GARLIC BUTTER

**½ garlic clove, finely minced**

**½ cup (1 stick) butter, softened**

**¼ teaspoon finely grated lemon zest**

**1 teaspoon fresh lemon juice**

**Pinch of salt**

**Freshly ground black pepper, to taste**

Mix the garlic with the butter until blended. Mix in the lemon zest, lemon juice, salt, and pepper. Cover and chill. Bring to room temperature before serving.

❯ **Makes about ½ cup.**

# OYSTER SLURPERS WITH MOJITO-MIGNONETTE

*Raw oysters are often served with a mignonette sauce made with vinegar, pepper, and shallots. This take on the classic sauce uses rice vinegar instead of red wine or champagne vinegar and crushed red pepper flakes instead of cracked black pepper. Some mint, lime, and rum join the shallots for a festive Caribbean feel.*

**1 dozen freshly shucked oysters, on the half shell with as much oyster liquor as possible reserved in the shell**

**Crushed ice**

**½ cup rice vinegar**

**2 tablespoons fresh mint leaves**

**¼ cup fresh lime juice**

**2 tablespoons minced shallot**

**¼ teaspoon crushed red pepper flakes**

**Ice cubes**

**4 ounces good-quality spiced rum or tequila**

**Thinly sliced jalapeño pepper rounds**

**Lime wedges**

Place the oysters on a large platter with a crushed ice base.

Muddle the vinegar, mint, lime juice, shallot, and crushed red pepper flakes together in shaker or mixing cup. Add ice cubes and the rum. Shake all together for 10 seconds, until just mixed and chilled.

Drizzle the rum mixture over the oysters. Place a jalapeño slice on each oyster. Serve with lime wedges, and use remainder of sauce for dipping.

❯ **Makes 6 servings.**

 Where I come from, men had to know how to cook steak, boil shrimp, fry fish, and shuck fresh oysters. Chicks thought it was cool, for one thing!

# SHRIMP PO' BOY

*KIX STORY:* There's a classic hole-in-the-wall place in my hometown of Shreveport that's been around since the 1930s. Herby-K's was originally called The Flying Crow, a place to get tobacco, liquor, and the occasional sandwich. In 1936, Herbert J. Busi Jr., decided to turn the liquor store into a restaurant and name it after himself. Herbie-K was a nickname he picked up when he was in college at Louisiana State University. In 1945, he put the Shrimp Buster sandwich with Secret Shrimp Buster Sauce on the menu, and the rest, as they say, is history. I've been a regular customer at Herbie-K's for years, but there's no way I would try to wrestle the Shrimp Buster sandwich or sauce recipe out of Miss Janet (Janet Bean is the current owner of Herbie-K's, along with her daughter and son-in-law, Angela and David Doe). There's nothing like it! I take anybody I can drag along with me to go eat one anytime I'm near Shreveport.

I'm not even trying to imitate the Herbie-K's Shrimp Buster with this recipe, but it is a solid shrimp Po' Boy recipe, and the Spicy Remoulade Sauce is pretty dang tasty.

**1 large loaf French or Italian bread**
**1/2 cup mayonnaise**
**Tomato slices, as many as you want**
**Shredded lettuce**
**Vegetable oil, for frying**
**1 cup yellow cornmeal**
**1 tablespoon KB's Shreveport Shake Seasoning (see recipe in chapter 6)**

**1 pint shucked oysters, drained (optional)**
**8 large shrimp, peeled and deveined**
**Spicy Remoulade Sauce (see recipe)**
**Revved-Up Brussels Sprouts Slaw (see recipe)**
**Hot pepper sauce**

Cut the loaf of bread in half crosswise, then slice each half open. Spread the mayo on both cut sides of the bread. Lay the tomatoes and shredded lettuce on the bottom halves.

Pour the oil into a large, heavy pot at least halfway up the sides, and heat over high heat to 360 degrees.

Combine the cornmeal and seasoning in a bowl. Add the oysters and the shrimp, and toss to coat evenly. Drop the shrimp and oysters into the hot oil in small batches. Don't crowd the pot. Turn frequently, and cook until golden brown, about 2 minutes. Drain on paper towels.

Place the oysters and shrimp on top of the lettuce and tomatoes. Dollop Spicy Remoulade Sauce and Revved-Up Brussels Sprouts Slaw on top. Season with hot sauce, and top with the top halves of the bread. Eat immediately.

❯ **Makes 2 big sandwiches or 4 to 6 servings.**

# SPICY REMOULADE SAUCE

½ cup chopped onion

½ cup chopped green onions

½ cup chopped celery

1 tablespoon chopped garlic

¼ cup chopped parsley

½ cup mayonnaise

2 tablespoons ketchup

3 tablespoons spicy brown or whole-
grain mustard

¼ cup lemon juice

1 tablespoon paprika

1 tablespoon smoked paprika

Salt, to taste

Pepper, to taste

Hot sauce, to taste

½ cup olive oil

Combine all the ingredients except the olive oil in a bowl. Slowly pour in the oil while stirring. Serve immediately or chill. The sauce keeps in the refrigerator for up to a week.

❷ Makes about 1 to 2 cups.

*KIX TIP:* If you want the perfect bread for a Po' Boy sandwich, you'll either have to go to New Orleans and buy some fresh French bread from a local bakery, move somewhere below sea level and bake some bread yourself, or order some New Orleans French bread online. I've had a couple of different chefs in New Orleans explain to me that the bread baked there is special because yeast rises differently below sea level. I'm not a chemist, but eating is believing!

# REVVED-UP BRUSSELS SPROUTS SLAW

*Coleslaw may be a Southern staple, but honestly, I consider it to be like the opening act at a big concert. You're gonna get some on the side of your entrée whether you want any or not, and you're really there for the main dish. That said, I love Brussels sprouts, so I figured turning them into a slaw would satisfy everybody: those of you who enjoy slaw with your barbecue and Po' Boys and me, who usually scrapes the slaw away from the good stuff!*

**1 to 2 pounds Brussels sprouts, finely chopped or shredded**

**1 large shallot, thinly sliced**

**¼ cup vegetable oil**

**½ cup white or rice vinegar**

**1 tablespoon salt**

**½ tablespoon mustard seed**

**1 teaspoon hot sauce or crushed red pepper flakes (optional)**

**¼ to ½ cup sugar, to taste**

Mix together the Brussels sprouts and shallots in a large bowl. In a saucepan blend together the oil, vinegar, salt, mustard seed, hot sauce, if using, and sugar. Bring to a boil over medium-high heat. Remove from heat, and pour over vegetables. Stir and let cool. Refrigerate.

❂ **Makes 4 to 6 servings.**

# GRILLED AND SMOTHERED STRIP STEAK

*KIX STORY*: As the host of *Steak Out with Kix Brooks* on the Cooking Channel, I had the incredible opportunity to travel across the country in search of the best steak houses. I visited all kinds of establishments, from traditional steak houses to modern restaurants pushing culinary boundaries. The number one thing I learned was that you have to start with a great piece of meat. USDA Prime is the highest grade of meat you can get. This is the grade of beef that contains the greatest degree of marbling, the flecks and streaks of fat in the meat. The more marbling you have, the more tender, juicy, and full of flavor the meat will be. USDA Choice beef has less marbling than Prime, but it is still very high quality, and it's the most popular grade as it's less expensive than Prime and more widely available. The number two thing I learned is that you shouldn't cook your steak immediately after buying it. Let it sit in the fridge for at least a couple of days to give the enzymes time to break down and release the most flavor.

*Instead of "out of the frying pan and into the fire," this recipe calls for the steak to go "out of the fire and into the frying pan." You'll be making your own steak sauce with this one as well. It's not hard to do, and the flavor rivals sauces that take way more time and effort. This recipe calls for strip steaks, which are also called New York strip, Kansas City strip, or strip loin. The "smother" is more of a sauce than a gravy.*

## Steak

- 4 (1½-inch thick) strip steaks (with or without bone—bone-in has the best flavor)
- 2 tablespoons canola oil
- ½ tablespoon sea salt
- 1 tablespoon freshly ground black pepper
- 2 tablespoons KB's Shreveport Shake Seasoning (see recipe in chapter 6) or other Cajun or Creole seasoning

## Smother

- 2 tablespoons bacon drippings or lard
- 2 tablespoons canola or vegetable oil
- 1 red bell pepper, roughly chopped
- 1 green bell pepper, roughly chopped
- 1 medium white or yellow onion, roughly chopped
- 2 garlic cloves, minced
- 1 cup beef broth
- ½ cup brewed black coffee
- 1 to 2 tablespoons hot sauce
- 2 tablespoons Worcestershire sauce
- 1 tablespoon KB's Shreveport Shake Seasoning (see recipe in chapter 6) or any Cajun or Creole seasoning
- 2 tablespoons ketchup
- 1 teaspoon salt

**1 teaspoon black pepper**

**2 tablespoons unsalted butter**

**1 tablespoon chopped fresh parsley, or
thinly sliced green onion, garnish**

To prepare the steaks to medium-rare, rub the steaks with canola oil, salt, pepper, and seasoning 1 hour before cooking. Let the steaks rest at room temperature.

Meanwhile, prepare the smother about 30 minutes before you're ready to cook the steaks. Heat the grill to medium. Place a cast-iron skillet on the grill grate, and add the bacon drippings and oil. Add the bell peppers and onion; stir and cook until the vegetables begin to soften, for about 5 minutes. Add the garlic, and cook for 3 minutes.

*KIX TIP:* I chose a strip steak for this recipe because I like the "tooth" of the strip. Instead of melting in your mouth as a filet mignon or rib eye would, a strip or Kansas City strip steak is slightly chewier, in a good way!

Add the broth, coffee, hot sauce, Worcestershire sauce, and seasoning, and bring to a low simmer. Add the ketchup, salt, and black pepper. Move the pot to lower heat, and simmer until the sauce thickens.

Place the steaks over direct heat (the hot area) on the grill; sear for 5 minutes. Flip the steaks, and sear the other side for 5 minutes. The steaks should now be done to medium-rare.

*KIX TIP:* A great accompaniment for this steak is asparagus. Don't be afraid to throw some asparagus right on the grill when you cook the steaks. Baste the asparagus with a little olive oil, and toss on a dash of salt and pepper. When you take the steaks off, just turn the fire down or close the vents on a charcoal grill, and leave the asparagus on the grill. When you're ready to serve your steaks, pull the asparagus off the grill. It should be the perfect texture, and besides being a great side, it looks great as a garnish. If you want to press your luck, do the same routine, but wrap six or eight pieces of asparagus with a strip of bacon and secure with a toothpick before putting it on the grill—awesome!

Stir the butter into the sauce, then remove steaks from grill, and place directly into the pan with the sauce. Remove the pan from the heat, and baste steaks with sauce for a couple of minutes.

Add the chopped parsley, and serve steaks and sauce at the table in the cast-iron skillet.

To prepare steaks indoors, sear on the stovetop in a hot skillet.

❯ **Makes 4 to 6 servings.**

 **Starting with a great piece of meat is like starting with a great song: you can't make a great record with a bad song.**

# REVERSE SEARED COWBOY CUT TOMAHAWK RIB EYE

*While searing is usually done at the beginning of cooking steak or other meat, this recipe calls for cooking the thick rib eye over indirect heat first, then searing at the end. Doing it this way allows the steak to cook consistently all the way through, and then when you sear it at the end, you get that nicely browned crust associated with a perfectly grilled steak. The reverse sear ensures that these steaks will be a consistent pink throughout, with a seared crust and no gray band around a red center.*

*Tomahawk Rib eye can be prepared by your butcher. This method leaves a long section of the rib bone attached, with the bone trimmed clean.*

**4 tablespoons freshly ground black pepper**

**3 tablespoons sea salt**

**1 tablespoon brown sugar**

**2 (1 1/2- to 2-inch thick) Tomahawk Rib eye Steaks (Prime or Choice)**

**1/4 cup olive oil**

**Fresh rosemary and thyme sprigs, soaked in water while steak is cooking**

Combine the pepper, salt, and brown sugar in a bowl to make a rub for the steak.

Two hours before cooking the steaks, massage them with the rub on all sides, reserving about 1/4 cup of the rub. Wrap the steaks in plastic wrap, and set aside to rest at room temperature.

While the steaks are resting, prepare the grill for direct/indirect cooking, which means having one hot side with the coals or gas flame and one cooler side with no direct heat. Place a cast-iron griddle over the direct heat, and allow griddle to get hot.

Unwrap the steaks, and brush on all sides with the olive oil. Sprinkle with the remaining rub. Place the steaks on the griddle over indirect heat. Allow steaks to cook slowly for about 20 minutes, and flip and cook for another 20 minutes (about 40 minutes total). Use an instant-read thermometer inserted into the thick part of the center of the steaks. When steaks are about 110 to 115 degrees, remove from grill and let rest on the cutting board for about 5 minutes. Trust the thermometer!

While steaks are resting, ensure the coals or flames are hot and the griddle is smoking hot.

Place the steaks on the hot griddle to sear. Place soaked rosemary and thyme sprigs directly on the griddle surrounding the steaks. The smoke from the herbs will bring a subtle flavor to the meat.

Sear steaks for 2 to 4 minutes on each side, depending on the size of the steak.

Check the temperature of seared steaks with the instant-read thermometer. For medium-rare, cook to about 135 degrees.

Transfer the steaks to a warmed serving platter and tent with foil. Allow the steaks to rest for 5 to 10 minutes before cutting.

If you don't have access to a grill, you can make these steaks indoors. Cook them in the oven at 350 degrees until internal temperature registers 110–115. Then sear the steaks in a hot skillet on the stovetop.

❷ **Makes 4 servings.**

# HONKY-TONK TEQUILA STEAK

*KIX STORY:* Ronnie Dunn and I burned up the road and the stage together for more than twenty years as Brooks & Dunn. A lot of the music we made was what you might call rambunctious, honky-tonk country—songs like "Boot Scootin' Boogie," "Little Miss Honky Tonk," "You Can't Take the Honky Tonk Out of the Girl," and "Honky Tonk Stomp"—you get the idea. This steak recipe is just as rowdy as those two-steppin' barroom tunes. It's easy to transport the marinating steak in a cooler to a picnic or tailgate party. Take it out of the cooler while you're setting up your grill, then slap it on the hot fire, and in less than 10 minutes, your steak is ready. Remember to bring a big cutting board for resting and slicing your steak on.

## Tequila Marinade

**Big handful of fresh cilantro leaves**

**1/4 cup tequila**

**1/2 cup fresh lime juice**

**1/4 cup Worcestershire sauce**

**1/2 teaspoon black pepper**

**1/2 teaspoon salt**

**2 teaspoons garlic powder or 4 minced garlic cloves**

**1 teaspoon onion powder or 1 shallot, roughly chopped**

**1 serrano or jalapeño pepper, seeded and roughly chopped (optional)**

## Steak

**1 flank steak**

**1 to 2 teaspoons salt**

**1 teaspoon freshly ground black pepper**

Mix the cilantro, tequila, lime juice, Worcestershire sauce, black pepper, salt, garlic powder, onion powder, and serrano pepper in a large ziptop plastic bag or plastic storage container. Add the steak. Seal the bag or cover the container, and refrigerate for several hours.

*KIX TIP:* Overall I'm not a huge fan of marinades. People say they enhance the flavor, but in my own experience and from what I learned hosting a Cooking Channel steak show, it's all about getting the best cut of meat in the first place. The big-time chefs I met on the show earn their money with the steak sauces they make from scratch. A Prime cut of steak plus a sublime sauce make a great steak. I'll give you a couple of ideas for making a great steak sauce in chapter 6. I'm breaking my own rule for this particular flank steak though, because I think this zesty marinade really does impact the flavor, especially if you poke a few holes in the steak before you put it in the marinade.

Heat grill to high. Remove the steak from refrigerator or cooler, and let sit on counter, in the marinade, for at least 30 minutes before grilling. Remove it from the marinade, and sprinkle both sides with the salt and pepper. Discard the marinade. Grill or broil the steak for 4 to 5 minutes on each side over direct heat. Remove from the heat, and let the steak rest for 5 minutes on a cutting board. Slice against the grain and serve.

❯ **Makes 4 servings.**

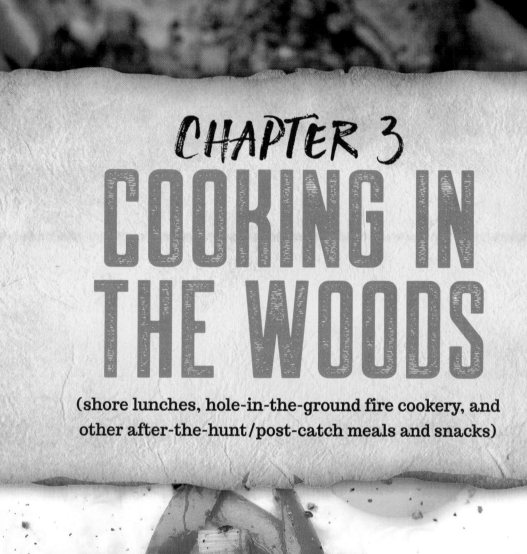

# CHAPTER 3
# COOKING IN THE WOODS

(shore lunches, hole-in-the-ground fire cookery, and
other after-the-hunt/post-catch meals and snacks)

# D-DADDY'S FISHING BOAT

*T*his chapter is about fishing and hunting and eating what you catch. I've also thrown in a recipe or two with regular ol' chicken and eggs and steak that you can cook up on your campfire or grill even if you're not a hunter or fisherperson. Whether it's a shore lunch on a salmon fishing trip to Alaska or an elk chili you whip up with some meat your neighbor gave you, it's gratifying to eat something that you know exactly where it came from. And if you, yourself, had a hand in catching it or bagging it, I swear it's gonna be the best thing you ever tasted!

My grandfather on my mother's side, the one we called D-Daddy, was confident in all things that he did as the mayor of his small town of Marion, Louisiana, owner of the general store there, and banker. It was when his suit came off and his fishing clothes went on that his smile was the widest though.

My mother died when I was only four years old, so I spent a lot of time with my grandparents. One day when I was with them, D-Daddy came home all excited. There was a lot of flooding from recent rains, and he had gotten the news about the bluegills (perch) biting like crazy down by the Ouachita River. So we loaded up and headed out.

We put our boat in at the edge of the water and started working our way through the flooded woods, fishing as we went, with cane poles and crickets for bait. Not much was happening, so we fired up our little three-horsepower motor and went deeper into the woods. It didn't take us too long to find the "honey hole"—*bam*! We started pulling in one bluegill after another. We even tied an extra line to the one already on our poles and started catching those fish two at a time—it was crazy! Bluegills are small compared to most fish, but these babies were big and fat. Man, we were having fun, laughing and catching fish and filling up our ice chest.

By the time the chest was full, it was getting close to dark, and D-Daddy said, "We need to head back." We packed up our poles and tackle box, he fired up the motor, and we started heading back through the trees. We hadn't gone too far when all of a sudden there was a loud *whackkk!* The boat bucked, and we were going nowhere. We looked at each other wide-eyed; I couldn't imagine what had happened, but I'm sure he already knew. D-Daddy pulled the motor up, and the propeller was completely gone. I had never before seen a look like that on his face, and it scared me. He obviously knew how far we had to

*Veggie Packets (page 49)*

go. No motor. No cell phone. It was almost dark. The water was deep and black.

In my seven-year-old wisdom I figured I could help, so I said, "I'll dive down and get it." I would have done anything to get that look off his face. I guess those words shook him out of it because he said, "No son, we'll take our time; it'll be alright," and we started paddling.

God gave us a nice moon that night, and for awhile we just paddled and worked our way through the trees. I'm not sure why, but after a while, he began to tell me stories about my momma, stories I had never heard before. He told me about how she had gotten sick with cancer, and he also told me about the things she had told him before she died.

D-Daddy had two daughters, my mom and her sister, my Aunt Grace. He talked about both of them, and then he told me about his son that had been born and died the same night, how the doctors had done something wrong, and how he had driven the baby, in a pouring Louisiana rain, all the way to the hospital in Baton Rouge some seven hours away to no avail. He wasn't blaming God for any of this, but he made some reference as to how all those things somehow led to us being together, and how it was important to focus on the blessings in life and not the hardships. It was a lot for my young heart to digest, but the wisdom has never left me.

Next thing you know, D-Daddy was smiling, and I looked up and yelled, "There it is!" And there it was, the shadow of his old pickup truck in the darkness, on the edge of the water. He knew where we were all along, and I think his only true worry was what my grandmother must be thinking. Needless to say, she was more than a little excited to see me run through that door. I didn't think she would ever stop hugging me. And I have to say, the fish we had for dinner have never tasted better than they did that evening. Like the saying goes, "It's not the destination; it's the journey that matters."

# VEGGIE PACKETS

*KIX STORY:* I really like Brussels sprouts, and you'll find a couple of recipes using them in this book. My second favorite vegetable is asparagus. This is a great way to cook asparagus, but it also works with root vegetables, like carrots and parsnips, as well as onions, peppers, and potatoes. Heck, if you're not doing this in the woods or at your campsite, clean out the crisper drawer and get creative!

*The idea here is to wrap whatever vegetables you have on hand into a foil packet, and toss that packet directly on the fire or hot coals or in an oven. These would be great to eat with Salmon-in-the-Fire (see recipe in this chapter).*

**Washed, trimmed vegetables of your choice**

**Salt**

**Pepper**

**Other spices**

**Olive oil or butter**

Lay a handful of veggies on a square of foil. Sprinkle with salt, pepper, and any other spices you like. Drizzle with olive oil or put a pat of butter in middle of vegetables. Wrap up the veggies. Place directly on your fire or hot campfire coals or in a 400-degree oven. Roast until tender.

❯ **Each packet serves 1 to 2.**

# SALMON-IN-THE-FIRE

*KIX STORY*: By now, you've probably figured out that I like to fish. I grew up fishing, and I still fish to this day. While I started out catching those little sun perch and bream with my dad and grandpa, these days it's fun to go big. One of my favorite places to go is Mission Lodge in Bristol Bay, Alaska, where you can catch Pacific salmon (five different species), rainbow trout, Arctic char, and northern pike among others. And this is where I've had one of my best-ever meals-in-the-woods, a true delicacy known as Salmon-in-the-Fire.

**Fresh salmon fillets**

**Salt**

**Black pepper**

**2 teaspoons of butter for each fillet**

**1 tablespoon brown sugar for each fillet**

Build your fire! In Alaska, the lodge has big iron kettles hidden out in the woods with grills on top that we use to cook with on days we want to have a "shore lunch." It works just as well to circle up some rocks and build a fire on the ground. Or, you could throw your fish on the grill, or even cook it in your oven at home.

   *Please note: You gotta know how to manage your fire. If that doesn't make any sense to you, I highly suggest you cook your fish in the oven.

   Lay each fillet skin side down on a big square of foil. Lightly season each fillet with salt and pepper. Pinch the butter into pieces, and lay them on top of the fish. Sprinkle brown sugar over each, basically covering the entire fillet with a layer of sugar. Wrap the foil loosely around each fillet, forming a packet. Pinch the foil together to tightly seal. If you're cooking outside with a real fire, double-wrap the fillets in foil. Place the packets directly on the hot coals, but not directly in the flames.

   Cook until fish is cooked. How long, you say? Well, it depends, but it could take 15 to 20 minutes. If your fire is smokin' hot, it might only take 8 to 10 minutes. Just check it along the way, and when it's firm and browned and smells good, it's ready! Oh yeah! This is some good eatin'! Best-ever campfire cuisine!

   *If you're cooking in the oven, set your temp at 425 to 450 degrees, and plan on it taking about 16 to 20 minutes.

*KIX TIP*: If you wanted to get fancy, you could add garlic, lemon, onions, Dijon mustard, mayonnaise, dill, or whatever you have on hand to the packet or spread it on the fish. But if all you have is sugar and butter, you will not be disappointed.

**KIX STORY:** Just when you've achieved some celebrity, a presence like Dale Earnhardt arrives in your life. Even at the height of Brooks & Dunn fame, I was always able to walk into the Walmart to buy razor blades or fly commercial airlines without any hassle. However, everyone wanted a piece of Dale, and, literally, people could not stay away from him. He and I became friends. Dale Earnhardt was like any grown man who refuses to let go of his third-grade dreams. Heavy equipment, hunting, the outdoors, and his family were the things he loved most in life.

Naturally Dale played rough, just like he drove his racecar. One Sunday after a race, he picked up my family and me in his jet. He flew us all down to San Salvador, an island that's part of the Bahamas. Dale had a 91-foot Hatteras yacht to sleep on and a 51-foot Hatteras fishing rig, called the *Intimidator* in honor of his nickname. The next day we woke up early for some deep-sea fishing.

If you've never been deep-sea fishing, you may not realize that a small tuna is actually much harder to pull in than a large mahi mahi or wahoo. My son, Eric, who was no more than six or seven at the time, learned that it's imperative to reel like your life depends on it if you don't want to end up with just a tuna fish head, nothing but mouth and eyeballs on your hook! The first time it happened, Dale smiled and responded to Eric's screams with, "Sharks! Reel like a man if you want the whole fish!" From that moment on, more times than not, Eric and I both won the entire fish as our prize!

By the end of this particular day, everyone but Dale was exhausted. We had a cooler full of fish, a great memory, and the sunburn to prove it. Believe it or not, there's a second part to this story, but I think I better save it for another time. I'll tell you this though, it involves a white marlin, bloody chum, and a practical joke that only Dale Earnhardt would dare play on anybody! Like I said, another story, another time. ☺

I don't have a freshly caught tuna recipe for you, but I do have another favorite freshly caught fish recipe to share. Fishing for redfish may not be as exciting as fishing for marlin or tuna with Dale Earnhardt, but it's still a challenge and fun. Redfish is caught

in the brackish water of South Louisiana. Brackish water is salt water and fresh water mixed together, so we're talking estuaries, mangroves, and marshes. When I was a kid, we'd head south and fish for redfish in the springtime. The skin of a redfish is so tough that the best way to deal with it is to grill the fish with the skin on. When it's done, the fish slides right off the skin.

# REDFISH ON THE HALF SHELL

**Freshly caught redfish**
**Mayonnaise**
**Salt**

**Pepper**
**Lemon wedges**

Heat the grill to medium.

Cut the whole fish in half, leaving the skin on. Spread the mayonnaise on top of the flesh side of the fish. Sprinkle with salt and pepper.

Place the fish on the grill, flesh side down, and grill for several minutes. Flip the fish over, scales side down, and grill for about 6 minutes, or until the skin is crisp. Remove from the grill and let it rest several minutes. The fish should slide right off the skin now. Squeeze the lemon on top of the fish before serving.

❯ **One fish typically serves 2 to 3.**

# SPICY WILD TURKEY TENDERS

*KIX STORY*: I really am a hunter-fisherman who likes to eat what I catch. Wild turkeys are fun to hunt, and one of my favorite ways to prepare the turkey is to cut the breast into tenders. A wild turkey's breast is not as big as that Butterball breast you get at the grocery store, and the taste is slightly different as well. I like to spice it up and fry it, but this oven-baked recipe is good when you're not in the mood for bringing out that big pot of oil. Of course you can substitute store-bought turkey or chicken for the wild turkey.

1 ½ cups all-purpose flour

2 teaspoons salt

2 teaspoons black pepper

½ teaspoon cayenne pepper, or to taste

2 eggs, beaten

⅓ cup milk

1 cup panko bread crumbs or any other dried bread crumbs, just make sure the crust is removed and the crumbs are small

1 cup unsweetened, shredded coconut

1 tablespoon paprika

8 to 10 wild turkey tenders or strips (1 ½–2 pounds)

Chopped chives and parsley, for garnish

Preheat the oven to 375 to 400 degrees.

Mix flour, salt, pepper, and cayenne in a bowl or plate. Mix eggs and milk together in a separate bowl. Mix panko, coconut, and paprika together in another bowl or plate.

Roll the turkey in the flour mixture. Dip into the milk mixture, shaking off the excess liquid. Then press into the bread crumb mixture, packing the mixture onto each piece. Do not shake off the crumb mixture.

Place the turkey onto a lightly oiled baking sheet. Bake about 40 minutes, turning over halfway through the baking time. Check often—depending on the oven, baking times may vary. The outside should be nicely browned and the inside juicy. The best way to test is to cut one of the strips in half to make sure it's done all the way through. If the tenders are thin, check at the 10-minute mark, as they will take less time than thicker pieces of meat.

These are delicious plain or served with a sweet chili sauce, honey mustard, ketchup, or even a ranch dip.

❯ Serves 4 to 6.

# GETCHA SOME DUCK GUMBO

*KIX STORY:* There are as many types of gumbo as there are cooks, and all Louisianans have their favorite gumbo recipe. Duck hunting is a favorite sport of mine, and I think one of the best ways to prepare duck is in a gumbo. The key, of course, is a good roux.

I grew up in North Louisiana not far from the Texas and Arkansas borders. People ask me if that's Cajun or Creole country. And honestly, I don't think it's either one. Up north, we have our own take on the classic dishes associated with Louisiana cooking, and many of those dishes start with a roux. I use peanut oil and flour to make mine, and I don't make it dark, dark brown. Instead, I like a nice caramel-colored roux, medium brown in color.

*Gumbo is a roux-based stew, which originated in southern Louisiana in the eighteenth century; it was first described in writing in the early 1800s. It combines ingredients and techniques from several cultures, including French, Spanish, German, West African, and Choctaw. You start with a roux, and then you add a variety of ingredients, which may include stock, meat or shellfish, vegetables, sausage, ham, spices . . . the list is endless really!*

**Enough vegetable oil to cover bottom of Dutch oven or heavy pot**

**2 ducks, cut into pieces (4 to 5 pounds total)**

**2 teaspoons KB's Shreveport Seasoning Shake (see recipe in chapter 6) or any Cajun or Creole seasoning**

**1 cup The Roux (see recipe)**

**2 cups chopped yellow onions**

**1 cup chopped celery**

**1 cup chopped green bell peppers**

**1/2 teaspoon salt**

**1/4 teaspoon cayenne pepper**

**1 pound andouille or other smoked sausage, cut into 1/4-inch slices**

**2 bay leaves**

**3 quarts chicken broth**

**2 cups cooked long-grain rice, wild or brown**

**2 tablespoons chopped green onions**

Heat the oil in a large Dutch oven or heavy pot over medium-high heat. Rub the duck pieces with Cajun seasoning, and then add them to the hot oil and cook until browned, 3 to 5 minutes on each side. Transfer to a plate and set aside.

Add the roux to the pot, heating it to a simmer. Add the onions, celery, bell peppers, salt, and cayenne. Cook, stirring constantly, until the vegetables are wilted, about 10 minutes.

Add the sausage and bay leaves, and cook, stirring, for 3 to 5 minutes. Stir in the broth, and bring to a gentle boil, then reduce the heat to low. Simmer, uncovered, for 1 hour. Add the duck, and simmer for another hour.

Remove the bay leaves, and skim off any fat that has risen to the surface. Serve in deep bowls with the rice. Garnish with green onions.

❷ **Serves 6 to 8.**

# THE ROUX

*Traditional Louisiana cuisine inherited the roux from the French. The roux is a staple ingredient used to thicken stews, sauces, gumbos, etouffées, and many things in between. Equal parts fat and flour are blended over heat to create a beautiful sauce of varying colors and consistency. Depending on where you are in Louisiana, roux can be made with butter, peanut oil, bacon drippings, lard, or even duck fat. The Creole roux is usually made with butter, while the Cajun roux is more likely to be made with oil.*

**1 cup peanut oil**                                    **1 cup all-purpose flour**

Heat a heavy skillet or cast-iron pot over medium heat. Add the oil. When the oil is hot, gradually stir in the flour, a couple of tablespoons at a time, stirring constantly until well blended. Reduce the heat to medium-low, and cook, stirring constantly, until the mixture turns a nice caramel color. The longer you cook it, the darker the roux will become. You must keep stirring; otherwise the roux will stick to the pan and that would ruin it. By the way, the darker the roux gets, the nuttier it will taste and the less it will taste like raw flour. So taste the roux as you're stirring it, and you can decide what tastes good to you.

This makes plenty of roux for a big pot of gumbo or etouffée. You can double or triple the recipe and store unused roux in the refrigerator for a few weeks.

You can use roux to thicken other dishes too, such as gravy or beans, simply by stirring a couple of tablespoons or so into the broth or vegetables while they're cooking.

## Heat and patience. That's all it takes to make the perfect roux.

# BACON-WRAPPED JALAPEÑO DUCK POPPERS

*KIX STORY*: The first time I ate duck with bacon was on a deer hunting trip with my dad when I was about six or seven years old. The duck hunters joined us deer hunters at the evening's campfire and cookout. They put duck breasts wrapped in bacon on the open fire, and man, talk about good eatin'!

If you ask me, the best ducks to eat are teal wood ducks, and it's all about the breast meat. So breast-out your ducks, and grab the bacon and cream cheese, and get ready for a mouthful of goodness.

1 pound bacon, with 3 slices set aside to make bacon bits

1 pound duck breast meat or chicken, cut into strips

Salt and pepper

1 (8-ounce) package cream cheese, softened

1/2 cup finely chopped shallots

12 jalapeño peppers, tops cut off and seeds removed

Vegetable oil

Preheat the oven to 350 degrees.

Lay all but 3 bacon slices in single layer on a baking sheet, and bake 20 to 30 minutes, until the fat is rendered but strips are not crispy. Remove from oven, and let cool while assembling the poppers.

Fry the remaining slices of bacon in a skillet over medium-high heat until extra crispy. Remove the bacon from skillet, reserving the bacon drippings. Set the bacon aside to cool, and then crumble it into bits.

Season the duck meat with salt and pepper on all sides. Reheat the pan over medium-high heat, and add the duck. Fry the duck, turning frequently, until done, for approximately 5 minutes. Remove the duck from pan, and drain on paper towels. When cool, cut the duck meat into small pieces or chunks.

*Kix Tip:* Mix it up a little, and use some small sweet peppers along with the jalapeño peppers. They'll be delicious, and if you have somebody in the crowd who's afraid of hot stuff, they'll be happy you thought of them. ☺

Mix the softened cream cheese, duck meat, bacon crumbles, and shallots together in a bowl until well combined. Taste and add more salt and pepper if needed or any other spices you like.

Using a spoon or your fingers, stuff each jalapeño pepper with the cream cheese mixture. Wrap a piece of the partially baked bacon around each pepper, securing with a toothpick. Lay the peppers on a lightly oiled baking sheet or stand them up in a jalapeño popper pan. Bake at 350 degrees until bubbling and bacon is crispy.

❍ **Makes 12 poppers.**

# "DON'T KNOCK IT 'TIL YOU TRY IT" SQUIRREL STEW

*KIX STORY*: I remember squirrel hunting at Papaw's place when I was a kid; I shot my first squirrel, skinned it, and threw it in the deep fryer with all the rest of the game the Whittington clan had harvested that day. We had fried squirrel for dinner; it was fantastic, and I never thought a thing about it. I tell that story to people now, and they look at me like I have antlers coming out of my head! Squirrel is really tasty fried, but it's also good in a stew. If you're more about feeding the squirrels in your yard than eating them for dinner, you can use rabbit to make this stew, or heck, chicken is good too!

2 tablespoons olive oil

2 ribs celery, cut into bite-size pieces

1 carrot, peeled, cut into bite-size pieces

1 small onion, chopped

Salt and freshly ground black pepper

1 (14 ½-ounce) can chopped tomatoes

1 (14-ounce) can chicken broth

1 tablespoon tomato paste

½ cup fresh basil leaves, torn into pieces

1 bay leaf

½ teaspoon dried thyme leaves

1 ½ to 2 pounds squirrel, rabbit, or chicken meat, on the bone

1 (15-ounce) can kidney beans, drained and rinsed

1 cup frozen corn kernels

Heat the oil in a large, heavy saucepan over medium heat. Add the celery, carrot, and onion, and cook until the onion is translucent, for about 5 minutes. Season with salt and pepper. Stir in the tomatoes with their juices, chicken broth, tomato paste, basil, bay leaf, and thyme. Add the meat, pressing it to submerge.

Bring the cooking liquid to a simmer. Reduce the heat to medium-low, and simmer gently, uncovered and stirring the mixture occasionally, until the meat is almost cooked through, for about 25 minutes. Using tongs, transfer the meat to a work surface, and let cool for 5 minutes. Discard the bay leaf. Add the kidney beans and frozen corn to the pot. Return to a simmer, and cook until the liquid has reduced to a stew consistency, for about 10 minutes.

Remove the bones from the meat, and discard the bones. Cut the meat into bite-size pieces. Return the meat to the stew, and bring to a simmer. Season with salt and pepper, to taste.

❯ Makes 8 to 10 servings.

*KIX TIP:* Crusty bread, biscuits, and Aunt Katty's Cheese Wafers (recipe in chapter 5) are good with this stew.

# KIX ON CAST IRON

I suggest using cast-iron cookware throughout this cookbook, and here's why: Cast iron is virtually indestructible, and its ability to retain heat makes it ideal for browning, searing, and frying. A cast-iron skillet, pot, or griddle can last a hundred years or more if you take care of it properly. It's not that hard to care for it either. Here's how:
Hand wash a cast-iron pan, and dry it immediately after washing.
Rub the pan with a light coat of vegetable oil after every wash. Use just enough oil to restore the sheen without being sticky.

Other cast iron tips:
You can use a little dish soap to scrub your cast iron. Just be sure to rinse, dry, and oil it immediately afterward.
Never put a cast-iron pan in the dishwasher.
You've probably heard about "seasoning" cast iron. Most new cast-iron pans you buy these days come already seasoned, but you can re-season the cookware anytime you need to. Here's how:
Wash the cast-iron pan with hot, soapy water and a stiff brush.
Rinse and dry completely.
Apply a very thin, even coat of melted shortening or cooking oil to the cookware inside and out.
Set the oven temperature to 350 to 400 degrees.
Place the pan upside down on top rack of oven. You can put foil or a large baking pan on the rack under the upside-down pan to catch oil drips.
Heat for at least 1 hour. Turn the oven off, and let the pan cool in the oven.
Store the pan uncovered in a dry place when cooled.
Re-season as necessary.

*KIX STORY:* For a number of years, I've been involved with Monroe Harding in Nashville. Founded as a Presbyterian Orphanage in the late 1800s, the organization provides a chance, and very often a home, for children and young people who have nowhere else to turn. When I say I've been "involved" with Monroe Harding, what I mean is, I visit occasionally and have been in charge of the yearly fundraiser in the past. One year, the group honored me with its "Volunteer of the Year" award. I was all puffed up with pride until a few moments before I received the award.

While I was waiting to be called up to the stage, a Monroe Harding alumnus spoke about how when he was there as a youth, a dentist came into his room one day and visited with him. After half an hour or so, the dentist asked the boy if he'd like to come and live with him. This was a 14-year-old boy the dentist barely knew, mind you, but the dentist offered, "Let's just give it a couple weeks, and if you're not comfortable in my family's home then I'll bring you back." The kid agreed and went home with the dentist. After about a week, the young boy told the dentist how much it meant that he had been invited to live in such a wonderful home, but he needed to go back to Monroe Harding. He told the dentist he was guilt-ridden because his roommate was back at the orphanage all by himself, and he just couldn't bear to leave him there alone.

Instead of taking the boy back, the dentist drove to Monroe Harding, picked up the roommate, and brought him home to live with the family too! I should add that this dentist had two teenaged daughters at the time. Can you even imagine? Two teenaged daughters, and you bring home two troubled teenage boys to live in the same house! The dentist saw that both of those boys got through high school, and he paid for their college tuition as well. The alumnus who spoke that morning was now the CEO of a major company. He called the dentist, who had become his surrogate father, up to the stage to receive the Donor's Award. In accepting the award, the dentist explained that the honor was all his to have had these two young men be such an important part of his life and to see them grow up to become moral examples and assets to their communities.

Perhaps you've heard that old story about the chicken and the pig talking about providing breakfast for the farmer. The chicken suggested bacon and eggs. The pig said, "Hey, chicken, for you it's a contribution; for me, it's a full commitment!"

Of course, I felt very embarrassed and very much like the chicken that day, but the impression the young man's and dentist's story made on me was profound.

Thanks for letting me tell this rather long story. It's a meaningful one for me, and now, whenever it's time to commit to something, I always ask myself, how deep can I go in? If I can only be the chicken, that's okay; I just can't pat myself on the back too hard if that's the case.

# CAST IRON STEAK AND EGGS

*Speaking of breakfast and eggs, try this one! It's an easy dish to make for breakfast or dinner, and it's a good one to throw down at the campsite or anywhere, anytime you have an outdoor fire going.*

**Thinly sliced steak**

**Salt**

**Pepper**

**Vegetable oil or butter**

**Eggs**

**Grated cheese**

**Tomatoes**

**Green onion, chopped**

**Fresh arugula (optional)**

Sprinkle the steak on all sides with salt and pepper. Heat a large cast-iron skillet over medium-high heat or on a hot campfire grate. Add the oil. When hot, add the steak. Brown the steak on one side, then flip and brown the other side. Stack the steak pieces on top of each other and push to the side of the skillet, or remove and wrap in foil while you fry the eggs. You can add more oil or butter to the skillet to fry the eggs in if needed.

Fry the egg in the hot pan. Once they're done the way you like them, lift them onto the top of the steak slices. Sprinkle cheese, tomatoes, green onion, arugula, and more grated cheese on top. Remove the skillet from the heat or fire, cover, and let sit for a few minutes. Serve directly from the skillet.

# ELK CHILI

*KIX STORY:* There seems to be a lot of debating in chili circles about beans and no beans, ground meat or cubed meat, and what's real chili and what's not. It's enough to make your head spin. Seems Texas was the likely birthplace of chili, but Cincinnati and other Northern cities have certainly put their spin on the dish. Bottom line, chili varies, depending on where you live and how your mama made it. My wife, Barbara, makes a mean Elk Chili, and she tells me that you can use your own favorite chili recipe and use elk instead of beef and do your own version of elk chili. Of course, you're welcome to follow this recipe!

1 tablespoon olive oil

1 pound elk meat, ground or cubed (or ground or cubed beef)

1 medium onion, chopped

1 red or green bell pepper, chopped

Pinch of salt

Pinch of black pepper

2 teaspoons chili powder

1 teaspoon ground cumin

1 teaspoon dried oregano

1 (15-ounce) can red kidney or chili beans

1 (12-ounce) bottle chili sauce

1 (14-ounce) can petite diced tomatoes

2 (15-ounce) cans beef broth

Garnish options: grated cheese, chopped onion, sour cream, etc.

Heat the olive oil in a large, heavy pot or Dutch oven over medium-high heat.

Add the meat to the hot oil. Stir in the onion and bell pepper, and sprinkle with salt and pepper. Cook until the meat is completely browned and vegetables are softened.

Add the chili powder, cumin, oregano, beans, chili sauce, tomatoes, and broth. Bring to boil, then reduce heat to low, and simmer for several hours. Serve with Aunt Katty's Cheese Wafers (recipe in chapter 5).

❯ **Makes 8 servings.**

*KIX TIP:* The thing about chili is that it's really hard to screw it up! You can add more beans or more tomatoes. You can add a can of green chilies. You can delete this or that. You can amp up the spices however you want. What I'm saying is "go for it!"

# CAMP GRILLED WINGS

*KIX STORY*: Chicken wings—NOT! Look, nothing against chicken wing eaters, but I prefer to eat! And gnawing on a bony little wing with barely any meat on it could cause a feller to starve to death! I mean, you're burning more calories in working to get a bite off that tiny piece of chicken than you actually get from the sliver of meat itself. I'm more inclined to eat some spicy chicken (or turkey) tenders with plenty of white meat, battered or breaded in a nice fluffy flour mixture (see Spicy Wild Turkey Tenders recipe in this chapter). But I was coerced, I mean *convinced*, to include a wing recipe in this book. Actually, if you're gonna bother to eat a wing, I would highly recommend these!

**3 to 4 pounds chicken wings, cut apart at joints, wing tips discarded**
**½ cup olive oil or melted butter**
**Hot sauce, to taste**

**Salt**
**Black pepper**
**⅓ to ½ cup teriyaki sauce**

Heat the grill to medium, or preheat oven to 375 degrees.

Place the wings in a large bowl. Drizzle the oil over the wings, add a few dashes of hot sauce, and generously sprinkle with salt and black pepper. Toss the wings to coat with oil and sauce. Let them sit for a bit while the grill or oven heats up.

Brush the top of the wings lightly with teriyaki sauce. You don't want to put on a thick coat of sauce because it could burn and that could ruin the flavor.

Place the wings on the hot grill in a single layer or on a large baking sheet in a single layer if you're cooking them in the oven. Cook, turning occasionally, until the chicken is well-done and crispy, about 20 minutes. Baste lightly with teriyaki sauce often.

*KIX TIP*: If you don't like teriyaki sauce, you can use hot sauce, Italian dressing, barbecue sauce, or whatever sauce you like. Don't be afraid to season the wings with cayenne pepper, garlic, or herbs; let your taste buds be your guide.

If you're doing these in the oven, turn the broiler on for the last several minutes to crisp up the skin of the wings. If you're doing these on the grill, you can pile them all up on top of each other once they're cooked and let them hang out on the cooler side of the grill until ready to serve.

Serve these with extra teriyaki and hot sauce on the side.

❯ **Serves 10 to 12.**

# VENISON JERKY

*KIX STORY*: I really enjoy traveling on my tour bus, and considering how many years and miles I've spent on the road, it's probably a good thing I like it. I have a refrigerator, a wine cooler, and an awesome espresso maker on the bus. I don't really "cook" on the bus per se, but I do have plenty of foods I like in the fridge and cupboards, and I make sandwiches and eat snacks while we're rolling down the highway. One of my go-to high-protein snacks is jerky. I always have beef jerky with me, but sometimes, when I've been deer hunting and had a chance to pull out the smoker, I'll have Venison Jerky onboard too!

*If you don't have fresh venison to make this jerky, you could always use beef flank steak.*

**4 tablespoons soy sauce**

**4 tablespoons Worcestershire sauce**

**2 tablespoons packed brown sugar**

**1/4 teaspoon garlic powder**

**1/4 teaspoon onion powder**

**2 tablespoons A-1 steak sauce**

**1/2 teaspoon crushed black peppercorns**

**1 teaspoon salt, or to taste**

**2 pounds venison or flank steak, cut into strips**

Combine the soy sauce, Worcestershire sauce, brown sugar, garlic powder, onion powder, steak sauce, peppercorns, and salt in a large bowl. Add the meat, and let it marinate overnight in the refrigerator.

Crank up the charcoal or electric smoker. Remove the meat from the marinade, and hang each strip over the rack in the smoker. Smoke overnight. Or spread strips on a rack in the oven, and bake at 160 degrees for 6 hours, turning over halfway through the cooking time.

❯ **Makes 1 pound.**

*KIX STORY*: My earliest memory of deer hunting was a trip I took with my father when I was only about six or seven years old. Before the trip, we talked about what it would be like going out in the woods and hunting and how we were going to be camping with friends and cooking outdoors; it all seemed very exciting! I remember him waking me up in the middle of the night so we could drive three or four hours to get to the camp up in Arkansas. When we got there, the other hunters were starting to amble around in a big open area. There were deer hanging in the air from makeshift butcher racks, skinned and field dressed. This was "big boy" stuff, and I was invited!

Whoever was in charge explained to my dad where we would be hunting, and then we took off for a long walk through the woods. I was working hard to keep up but I didn't mind, I was happy to be on the hike. Dad would occasionally look over his shoulder and smile, but he was moving on really fast. Eventually he stopped and sat down next to a tree. These were deep woods, mind you, with no open ground anywhere, but there was a lane, maybe ten feet wide and about fifty yards long, where we would have a clear shot. My father had a twelve-gauge shotgun; I remember him showing me the end of the shell, which had a single ball in it. Most people hunt deer with rifles, but he explained this was close quarters, and a rifle bullet could travel a long way and could be very dangerous with this many people in the woods.

We sat quietly and waited and listened without talking. That morning there was no place in the world that I would rather have been, and it was probably the first time I realized how exciting it is to be around when the woods come alive. It went from dead quiet to the birds chirping, and then the squirrels started running around gathering up acorns. At one point a skunk walked across our shooting lane about twenty five yards in front of us. I wanted to scream, "A SKUNK!" and I'm sure my eyes were wide with panic, but my father just looked down and smiled, like, "cool huh?" Then, like a perfect picture out of a book, at the end of the lane, there was a deer. It poked around and looked up like it heard something. I was frozen. I glanced up and my dad had already shouldered his gun and was looking down the barrel; this was it! I was ready for the blast. The deer looked around again and either caught our scent or just didn't like the feeling it was getting and bounded away. I couldn't believe it! We had come all this way and had been waiting in the cold in our special place for this very moment . . . and nothing. What had happened?

I finally whispered to my dad, "Why didn't you shoot?" My father lowered his gun and patted me on the back. "It was a doe, a young doe, and we're not shooting them," he said. That was my first lesson in the difference between killing and "harvesting."

That evening we had a big cookout, and there was nothing wrong with the fact we didn't kill a deer. With all the stories that came with the day's hunt, my father got the same nod as the rest of the guys telling the story of how we had seen a young doe and let it go. The meat we ate was amazing; we had chicken fried venison, which I think was my favorite, plus corn on the cob, beans, and cornbread. Some duck hunters also brought duck breast they wrapped in bacon and put on an open fire; I think I ate my weight in those that night. The whole trip was a game changer; this hunting thing was awesome, and I was hooked!

By the way, real hunters are responsible about the way they do things. Sometimes there are so many does in an area that they starve to death, and if that's the case, it's responsible to take them. Generally, I will harvest a deer a season to have venison to eat—steaks and sausage as well as ground meat for chili. We have a program in Tennessee to feed the hungry, and I have a lot of friends who love the woods and will always harvest their limit and donate the meat to feed those in need.

# VENISON SALAMI

*This homemade venison salami is reminiscent of a summer sausage and is a delicious snack by itself or with crackers, cheese, and stone-ground mustard.*

**5 pounds ground venison or lean, ground beef**

**5 tablespoons Morton Tender Quick salt (There is no substitution for this salt. You can order it online or usually find it at sportsmen's stores.)**

**1 teaspoon hickory smoke salt (see Kix Tip)**

**2 ½ teaspoons garlic salt**

**2 ½ teaspoons freshly ground black pepper**

**2 ½ teaspoons mustard seed**

Mix the venison, salts, black pepper, and mustard seeds together in a very large glass or metal bowl until well blended.

Cover and refrigerate for 4 days. Each day, pull out the mixture, remix it, and then return it to the fridge.

At the end of the fourth day or on the fifth, preheat the oven to 250 degrees. Form the mixture into long rolls, approximately 2 ½ inches in diameter. You should have at least 4 salami logs. Bake the logs on a baking sheet for 4 hours. Remove from the oven, and chill immediately in the refrigerator.

Wrap the chilled salami in plastic wrap or waxed paper, and store in refrigerator for up to four weeks. Salami may be frozen and will keep for up to three months.

❯ **Makes 4 salami rolls.**

*KIX TIP:* If you can't find hickory smoke salt in the spice section of your local grocery store, you can use ½ teaspoon regular salt and ½ teaspoon smoked paprika. The Morton Tender Quick salt is a must though; it contains salt, sugar, and other curing agents. If you can't get this salt, you'll have to skip this recipe.

# CHAPTER 4
# CELEBRATE! WITH FOOD

(spreads for all occasions from holiday meals
to simple good-time get-togethers)

# CELEBRATE! WITH FOOD

*F*ood tied in with an activity might just be my very favorite way to eat. Nothing against fine dining where the focus is on the carefully prepared meal and the fine wine and all that. Don't get me wrong—I love *all that!* But those special occasions aside, I'm all about a culture where food and cooking is part of whatever event is going on, where everybody's all up in the middle of it.

That can certainly be the case for holiday meals. At my house, we tend to have a crowd for Thanksgiving, and instead of everybody showing up just in time to eat, we invite everyone to show up early and get in on the action. While I'm working on the turkey, Barb's making the stuffing, and my daughter, Molly, is baking the pie, and we recruit the others to help cream the onions, whip the cream, and set the table. That's just one holiday and one example, but I think you get the idea.

Of course if the weather cooperates and you can cook and eat outdoors for a springtime shrimp boil, a Cinco de Mayo party, or an "any Sunday" afternoon backyard hang, that's even better. I moved my TV outside to the patio so I could watch ballgames and NASCAR races while I'm grilling, and I love it when company joins me out there. We can visit, catch up, and watch the game or the race, and hopefully one of us keeps an eye on the food so it doesn't burn up completely.

Tailgating is another great example of an activity tied in with food. It's not just about eating but about getting fired up for the football game or the concert or whatever event you're headed to.

I wanted this chapter to be a source where you could find all the recipes you needed to throw a party or put out a nice holiday spread. These "spreads" will work great if you do everything suggested, but what I'm really hoping is that you'll be inspired to create celebration meals of your own and put your own spin on things. More than anything, I want the focus to be on creating memories with the people you love most.

# RED BEANS AND RICE

*KIX STORY*: You might have figured out by now that I like the "eating" part as much as the "cooking" part of this whole food game. Most of the time, I'm not willing to spend days on end coming up with the gourmet version of my favorite things to eat. But this recipe for New Year's Red Beans and Rice that's been passed down for at least a couple generations in my family is a case where you've got to take the time to do it right. It's worth it too—not only because it tastes so dang good but because it makes your house smell good for days. This is a two-and-a-half- to three-day ordeal:

Soak one night
Prepare the next night
Serve it the third night

*This makes a big batch of beans. You can freeze any that you don't eat, or you can cut the recipe in half and make a smaller batch.*

*Like the recipe name implies, we time it out so we can eat this dish on New Year's Day. A lot of Southerners swear by black-eyed peas for New Year's luck, but I get mine from red beans.*

**2 pounds dry red kidney beans, rinsed and picked over**

**1/2 pound salt pork**

**6 fist-sized ham hocks, or more**

**3 or 4 onions, diced**

**1 bunch green onions, chopped**

**4 ribs celery, sliced diagonally**

**1 1/2 to 2 cups diced green bell peppers**

**1 1/2 to 2 cups diced red bell peppers**

**2 or 3 fresh tomatoes, diced**

**2 (28-ounce) cans whole, peeled tomatoes, plus juice from one of the cans**

**1 (29-ounce) can tomato sauce**

**4 to 6 heads garlic or garlic powder, enough to cover the whole top of the bean pot**

**3 tablespoons Tabasco, or more**

**3 tablespoons Worcestershire sauce**

**1 teaspoon crushed red pepper flakes**

**1 tablespoon cumin**

**1/2 tablespoon dried oregano, or more**

**1/2 teaspoon thyme**

**1 teaspoon black pepper**

**1 (15-inch) roll pepperoni, sliced and quartered into 3/4-inch chunks**

**3 (10-inch) kielbasa sausages**

**3 (10-inch) smoked beef sausages**

**1 (1-pound) package hot Italian sausage links, casings removed and browned separately (optional)**

Soak the beans overnight in enough water to cover.

The next day, add the salt pork and ham hocks and more water to cover the beans. Cook over medium heat until the beans are beginning to soften, for about 1 ½ hours. Add more water if necessary.

*KIX TIP:* I add most of the spices to taste, so the amounts I've given are suggestions. During the cooking process, I taste and add more of this or that. You'll notice there's no salt added. You probably won't need any since the ham hocks, salt pork, and sausages bring a lot of salt into the dish already.

Add the onions, celery, bell peppers, fresh and canned tomatoes, tomato sauce, garlic, Tabasco, Worcestershire sauce, red peppers flakes, cumin, oregano, thyme, black pepper, pepperoni, kielbasa, and smoked sausage. Cook 1 hour, then add the browned Italian sausage, if using. Cook, uncovered, at least 2 more hours. Turn off stove, cover the pot, and let it sit out overnight.

The next day, cook the beans for a few more hours over low. If I'm home, I cook the beans on and off all that day, especially if I need to boil off some liquid. Serve over rice.

❷ **Makes about 24 servings.**

*KIX TIP:* Barb and I usually start cooking this late in the afternoon on the second day after soaking the beans. We cook it pretty much continuously until we go to bed. I don't refrigerate it until the third night.

# BEANS AND GREENS

*KIX STORY:* It's a Southern tradition for folks to eat black-eyed peas, collard greens, and hog jowl on New Year's Day. There are all kinds of stories as to why it's lucky to eat the peas and why you have to eat all three for the luck to stick, etc. Heck, I always eat red beans on New Year's, and I've had my share of good luck in this life, for which I'm forever grateful. If you want to use black-eyed peas in this recipe just to be safe, do it! If you're feeling a bit risky, try another kind of bean. Sometimes it's fun to roll the dice.

**1 or 2 ham hocks or hog jowl**

**4 (15-ounce) cans white beans, cannellini beans, or black-eyed peas, undrained, or 1 pound dry beans prepared from scratch (see Beans from Scratch recipe)**

**1 tablespoon olive oil, vegetable oil, or bacon drippings**

**1 onion, chopped**

**1 (32-ounce) bag greens, collard, mustard, or kale or a combination**

**¼ cup water**

**Crushed red pepper flakes**

**Salt**

**Black pepper**

**Squeeze of fresh lemon juice**

If you're using canned beans, you'll need to brown the ham hocks separately. Heat a skillet with olive oil, vegetable oil, or bacon drippings over medium-high heat until it's sizzling. Add the ham hocks and cook until brown on all sides.

Place cooked or canned beans in a large pot over low heat. Add the browned ham hocks. Let the beans cook while you prepare the greens.

Heat the oil in a large skillet over medium-high heat. Add the onions, and cook until softened and golden brown. Add the entire bag of greens to the pan. (You might need to add half the greens and let them wilt before adding the rest.) Reduce the heat to low or medium-low. Add the water, a pinch of crushed red pepper flakes, salt, and pepper. Cover and cook, stirring the greens occasionally to make sure they're not sticking to the pan or drying out. You can add more oil and more water if you need to, but only add a little bit at a time. You don't want to boil the greens. Instead you're steaming or sautéing them until they're softened and wilted. Once they're wilted, add a squeeze of fresh lemon.

Using a slotted spoon or tongs, remove the greens from the pan, and add to the pot of beans. Stirring occasionally, cook the beans and greens over low heat until completely warmed throughout.

Serve with cornbread (see Jalapeño-Corn Muffins recipe in chapter 5) or hot biscuits (see Angel Biscuits recipe in chapter 5).

**Serves 8 to 10.**

# BEANS FROM SCRATCH

**1 pound dried white or navy beans,
  rinsed and sorted**

**4 to 8 cups chicken or vegetable broth
  or water, or combination of both**

**Bacon, ham hock, or hog jowl**

**1/2 onion, diced**

**Salt**

**Black pepper**

Place the beans in a large pot, and cover completely with water. Bring to a boil over medium-high heat. Boil for 2 minutes, then remove from heat and let stand for 1 hour.

Rinse the beans again, and return to the pan. Cover with broth or water or a mixture of both. Make sure beans are completely covered by a couple of inches. Bring beans to a boil over medium-high heat, then reduce the heat to low and simmer.

While the beans are simmering, fry the bacon in a skillet until crispy. Remove and drain on paper towels. Add the onion to the bacon drippings in the pan, and sprinkle with salt and pepper. Sauté the onion until soft. Pour the onion and bacon drippings into the simmering beans. Season with salt and black pepper, at least 1 teaspoon of each.

If you're using a ham hock or hog jowl instead of bacon to flavor your beans, you can brown the ham hock or hog jowl and add it to the beans or just add it directly to beans without browning. You can add crumbled bacon to beans before serving.

**❍ Makes 8 servings.**

# CLASSIC SHRIMP BOIL WITH CORN AND RED POTATOES WITH SPICY BUTTER

*KIX STORY*: When I was a kid, we fished for shrimp in the spring, so this is a wonderful springtime feast, perfect for a Sunday afternoon picnic in the backyard or even an Easter dinner for the family.

One of the easiest and best things to cook is boiled shrimp. Heck, you don't even need hot grease for a shrimp boil! You can even get premade Shrimp Boil seasoning packets at the grocery store and follow the instructions, which is basically adding the Shrimp Boil to hot water, along with some lemon and extra spice if you like. When the shrimp float, peel and eat. It's that easy.

When I was in college and making the trip to South Louisiana for fresh oysters was no big deal, those oysters were a great add-on to a Shrimp Boil. So I suggest trying that too. Just remember to let somebody with a wire mesh glove deal with the shucking. Throw some small red potatoes in the boiling water first, and you'll have even more time to tell some lies while the shucking is happening. Potatoes like those Shrimp Boil spices. Heck, it's a great spice combination for a lot of things.

Once you've got everything boiled, a picnic table covered in newspaper or brown paper makes for easy cleanup. Yeah, I'm saying toss your boiled potatoes, oysters, corn, shrimp, whatever, right onto the paper and dig in!

Like I say, you can buy a complete Shrimp Boil seasoning mix at the store, and it's gonna taste great, but you can also whip up a fine shrimp boil yourself. Just keep reading this recipe. I grew up eating Gulf Shrimp, and they're still the greatest, so try to get some if you can.

*Cold beer pairs very well with this spread.*

**Shrimp**
4 to 5 quarts water
1 (12-ounce) can beer (optional)
½ cup Old Bay seasoning
2 lemons, cut in half

2 large onions, peeled and cut in half
4 garlic cloves, smashed
2 tablespoons salt
3 pounds small red potatoes, scrubbed
8 ears fresh corn, shucked and broken in half

**3 pounds large unshelled shrimp, tails on**

## Spicy Butter

**1 cup melted butter**

**Hot sauce, your favorite brand or try Kickin' It Hot Sauce (see recipe in chapter 6)**

**Lemon wedges, for serving**

Bring the water, beer, and Old Bay seasoning to a boil in a 10- to 12-quart pot over high heat. Squeeze juice from the two lemons into the water, then add the lemon halves, onions, garlic, and salt to the water.

Add the potatoes to the pot, and reduce the heat to low. Simmer, covered, until potatoes are almost tender, about 10 minutes. Add the corn, and cook 5 minutes more.

*KIX TIP:* You could also grill your corn on the side if you want. Toss it on the grill in the husk, and once it's nice and brown, it's done. Pull back the husk, and butter the corn or sprinkle salt and pepper on it. Cut it off the cob if you'd like.

Stir in the shrimp, pushing them completely into the water. Cover partially, and let stand until shrimp are cooked through, about 3 minutes. When the shrimp float, they're done. Ladle 2 cups of the broth into a glass measuring cup, and set aside. Drain the shrimp and vegetables through a large colander, discarding the remaining broth.

To make the Spicy Butter, stir the butter and hot sauce (to taste) together in a small saucepan. Divide the butter among small bowls or ramekins.

Transfer the shrimp and vegetables to a large platter or toss onto large brown paper spread over a table. Serve with Spicy Butter, lemon wedges, and reserved broth in bowls for dipping.

❷ **Makes 8 to 10 servings.**

# DALE'S SAUTÉED SHRIMP

**KIX STORY:** This is a story and a recipe all rolled into one. It's a fun story, though, about my very special friend, the late NASCAR racer Dale Earnhardt. I call the recipe Dale's Sautéed Shrimp, and if you keep reading you'll understand why. This is a great, fast recipe you can whip out when the fresh shrimp arrive. Call over the neighbors and dig in!

One of the coolest things I ever experienced with food was, believe it or not, at the Charlotte Motor Speedway. Dale Earnhardt Sr. had invited my wife, Barbara, and me to come watch him race. We joined his sister and his daughter Kelly in his luxurious suite at the racetrack and watched him "trade paint" all day.

Barbara and I had seen Dale win more than once at Charlotte and had even been in the middle of the chaos and spraying of champagne in the Winner's Circle with him before. I gave him one of my favorite cowboy hats in the Winner's Circle at one race, and he gave me the ball cap he was wearing—a ball cap that I still have. But this day was different; he blew out a tire and had been pushed back a couple of laps, and he and Rusty Wallace had been banging back and forth against each other all afternoon. I mean, he still managed a Top Ten finish, but I didn't expect him to be in a great mood, and I certainly wasn't expecting a great party, as we waited for him to put away his car and join us in the suite for a drink.

Most of the fans had gone, and Barb and I were about out of small talk, when I saw Dale come running across the racetrack, headed for the grandstand. He still had his racing suit on, pulled halfway down with a #3 t-shirt showing underneath and the arms of his fire suit tied around his waist. But what caught my eye was a plastic bag he was carrying. He looked up toward the suite as he was running and held up the bag to us, as if he were saying, "Hey, look what I got!" His wife, Teresa, was in the suite now, and I asked her, "What is that?" and she said, "No telling."

Now here was a guy who'd been running 190 miles an hour for about three hours. He'd had a wreck that would have put most of us in the hospital. He'd been banging on bumpers and getting hammered on in a way that would send most hot heads from L.A. into major road rage, and he came busting through the door of his suite grinning from ear to ear! He held up the bag and said, "FRESH SHRIMP, MAN!!!" I'm telling you, he was fired up! There were a few key things in his fridge like garlic and onions. He also had a little olive oil and some salt and pepper. He got that oil popping in a skillet on the stove and threw in the shrimp. He diced up some onion, minced some garlic, and hit the shrimp a couple of times with salt and pepper.

My mouth was watering, and about that time, the door swung open and in strolled Rusty Wallace. *Uh-oh,* I thought. After what I'd seen out of those two on this particular afternoon, I was thinking this could get ugly. But Rusty said, "Hey man, what've you got there?" Dale said, "Hey, Iron Head [a name Dale gave Rusty after he spun him out and almost killed him one year at the Daytona 500], fresh shrimp! Want some?" To which Rusty replied, "Damn right!"

I thought, *This is awesome*, and I finally asked Dale, "Where did those come from anyway?" He replied, "Some dude who flew up from the Gulf for the race. I talked him out of 'em. They're good, huh?" I honestly had never had sautéed shrimp in a pan before. As we were chomping away, I realized how easy it would be to add sautéed shrimp like that to pasta or rice, and how you could season them with any combination of spices and veggies to taste. So as much fun as getting the big pot of shrimp boil going, it doesn't have to be that way. You could just do what my dear friend Dale did and feed the whole gang.

*KIX STORY*: Anybody who knows me knows I love any kind of Mexican or Tex-Mex food. More likely than not, it's what I'm eating backstage after a performance. This is also the kind of spread I like to throw out for any big get-together at the house or down at my farm. It's especially festive for a Cinco de Mayo party or a Memorial Day weekend celebration. Heck, it's also a great reason to get outside after a long, cold winter. A three- to five-pound pork shoulder will serve six to ten, and if you have more guests than that, get a bigger piece of meat. Serve these Carnitas-Style Tacos with beans, guacamole, and salsa on the side and everybody's happy.

# KIX'S CARNITAS-STYLE TACOS

3- to 5-pound pork shoulder (also called pork "butt"), bone-in is fine since the bone will slide right out after it's cooked

Handful or two of James' Famous Pork "Butt" Rub (see recipe)

1 tablespoon salt

1 tablespoon freshly ground black pepper

½ onion, roughly chopped or sliced

1 (6-ounce) can tomato paste

1 (12-ounce) can root beer or beer of any kind

½ cup packed brown sugar

Chopped cilantro

Green onions, chopped

Lime wedges

Sour cream

Warm tortillas

Chopped fresh or pickled jalapeños

Queso fresco

Hot sauce

Guacamole

Warm tortillas, flour or corn or both

Preheat the oven to 300 degrees.

Trim any extra fat off the pork, but leave the fat cap on if you want. The fat cap is that harder, thicker white layer of fat. Some people think leaving it on brings out more flavor in the meat, but this pork will turn out great with or without the fat cap.

Rub the rub all over the pork. And when I say "rub the rub," I mean *rub the rub*. Rub it in well, making sure the meat is well-coated on all sides. Then rub in the salt and pepper. If you need more than a tablespoon of each to get the meat covered, use more. Obviously, this is a hands-on deal.

Place the onion in the bottom of a large, heavy ovenproof pan. Place the pork on top of the onion. Scrape the tomato paste into the pan, putting dollops all around the meat. Pour in the root beer. Press the brown sugar on top of the meat.

*KIX TIP:* If you're taking your pork directly out of the freezer, you don't even have to defrost it before you rub it with spices. You can "rub in the rub" and pop that puppy directly into the oven, and cook it a bit longer. You know it's done when the meat falls apart or the bone comes out easily.

Put the lid on the pot or cover tightly with foil. Roast the meat for about 3 hours, until the bone is loose and you can pull it out easily. This could cook all day on a lower temperature, on the side of your grill, over a campfire, or even in a slow cooker.

You can test it every hour or so and baste the pork with the liquid in the bottom of the pan if you want. You can even turn the roast over every now and then, but you don't have to do that.

Once cooked and tender, remove the pork from oven and let it sit for 20 minutes. Shred the meat with two forks, or just chop it into small pieces with a knife. The point is to get the meat into nice bite-size pieces, not too small, just a nice chunk that a person with a regular-sized mouth can easily eat! Pile the shredded pork onto a big platter and spoon pan juices from the cooked pork over the pile. Top with some chopped fresh cilantro, green onion, and a squeeze of fresh lime, then serve with warmed tortillas, more cilantro, onion, lime, sour cream, sliced jalapeños, Queso fresco, hot sauce, and guacamole.

❷ **Makes 8 to 10 servings.**

# JAMES' FAMOUS PORK "BUTT" RUB

*This rub was developed by a friend of mine named James. It will keep in your cupboard for at least a year. This rub is used in Kix's Carnitas-Style Tacos and is also great on pork tenderloin, roasted chicken, and steak. The recipe calls for ground chili pepper, which is different than chili powder. Chili powder is a mix that includes dried ground chili peppers along with cumin, garlic, and oregano. Ground chili pepper is just that—dried chili peppers that are ground up.*

**1 tablespoon salt**

**1 teaspoon celery salt**

**2 tablespoons garlic powder**

**2 tablespoons finely ground oregano**

**2 tablespoons cumin**

**1 tablespoon cinnamon**

**4 tablespoons ground chili pepper
(not chili powder)**

**½ teaspoon cocoa powder
½ teaspoon cayenne**

Mix together the salt, celery salt, garlic, oregano, cumin, cinnamon, ground chili pepper, cocoa powder, and cayenne in a jar with a lid. Shake to blend.

❯ **Makes approximately ¾ cup.**

# TACO TIME BEANS

*Skip the canned refried beans and make these. You can make them totally from scratch (see the Beans from Scratch recipe on page 84), substituting dried pinto beans for the dried white or navy beans. Or you can use canned pinto beans with excellent results. You can use 1 to 2 (4-ounce) cans roasted green chilie peppers if you don't want to roast your own. You can also add in fresh, chopped jalapeño, serrano, anaheim, poblano, or whatever your favorite pepper is for a little heat.*

*The thing about these beans is that you can double the recipe, and you can adjust all of the other ingredients to your own taste. It's a good idea to taste as you add the spices and pepper and lime juice so that you get it the way you like it.*

3 (15-ounce) cans pinto beans, drain 1 can and leave juice in other 2 cans, or use the whole batch of Beans from Scratch recipe

1/4 onion, chopped small

1 bunch of cilantro, coarsely chopped

Freshly ground black pepper

1 to 2 teaspoons cumin

2 tablespoons freshly squeezed lime, or more

1 small to medium roasted green chilie pepper, diced

Chopped green onion

Sour cream or Cotija cheese

Preheat the oven to 250 degrees.

Pour the beans into a big ovenproof pot, stir in onion, one-third of the cilantro, black pepper, cumin, 1 tablespoon of the lime juice, and the diced pepper.

Bring the beans to boil over medium-high heat. Reduce the heat to low, and simmer about 30 minutes. Put the lid on and put in the oven to bake. (You could put the pot of beans on the grill or campfire, and let them simmer as long as you want.) Keep them warm until serving time. Check occasionally and add 1/4 cup or so of water to keep them moist if needed. Don't let them dry out completely. Squeeze more lime juice over the beans before serving, and add fresh cilantro, chopped green onion, and a dollop of sour cream or Cotija cheese on the top.

❯ **Makes 8 servings.**

# KB'S LEMON-CILANTRO GUACAMOLE

*KIX STORY*: Fajitas, tacos, enchiladas—they're all delicious and especially so with some fresh guacamole on the side. What I've learned about guac is that it's all about the avocados. If they're too soft or too hard, they're no good. And if you open one up and it's too dark, it's bad. You want them just a little soft. I think the fresh cilantro is key to this guac, and in case you hadn't figured it out yet, dicing is therapy; it's a great way to work off your stress, so get to chopping! Here's my very easy-to-make guac recipe. Buen Provecho!

4 avocados

1/2 lemon, juiced (yes, lemon, not lime, for this guac)

Handful of fresh cilantro, chopped

1/2 white onion, diced or coarsely chopped (I like my onions chunky but you can cut yours smaller if you want)

Sea salt, to taste

A dollop of your favorite salsa (optional)

1 to 2 teaspoons pickled jalapeños, with a bit of pickling juice from the jar

Peel the avocados, and remove the pits. Put the pulp into a large bowl, and add the lemon juice, cilantro, onion, salt, salsa, if using, and jalapeños and juice. Mash well. I usually mash mine with a potato masher, but you could use a fork to get it to your favorite consistency.

❯ **Makes 8 servings.**

*KIX TIP*: To pick the perfect avocado, gently push your finger near the stem area. If it indents slightly, the avocado is ripe and ready to eat. If it's still too hard, put the avocado in a brown paper bag and leave on counter for a day or two; it will ripen right up.

# BARB'S HOMEMADE SALSA

2 cups chopped tomatoes

1/4 cup chopped red onion

1/4 cup chopped yellow onion

2 tablespoons canned green chilies or
  fresh jalapeño or both

2 tablespoons fresh lime juice

2 tablespoons chopped fresh cilantro

2 garlic cloves, peeled and minced

1 teaspoon ground cumin

1/4 teaspoon salt

In the bowl of a food processor, place the tomatoes, red onion, yellow onion, green chilies, lime juice, cilantro, garlic, cumin, and salt. Pulse until combined but still chunky. Transfer the salsa to a bowl, cover with plastic wrap, and refrigerate for at least 1 hour. If you don't have a food processor, you can use a blender, or you can chop everything up into smaller pieces and simply mix by hand.

❯ Makes 10 to 12 servings.

*KIX TIP:* This spread calls for a nice bucket of beer, perhaps Corona or a nice Northwest Craft IPA. If you want a big punch bowl of fun, mix up my Sangaritas (see recipe in chapter 8), which pair perfectly with all things Tex-Mex!

# NEXT-DAY NACHOS

Corn chips

Shredded cheddar or Mexican blend
  cheese

Leftover Carnitas Taco pork, shredded
  (see Kix's Carnitas-Style Tacos
  recipe in this chapter)

Leftover Taco Time Beans (see recipe
  in this chapter)

Chopped tomato

Sliced green onion

Sliced pickled or fresh jalapeños

Cilantro

Preheat the oven to 400 degrees.

    The key to making nachos that have all the ingredients distributed all the way through the layers is to start with a single layer of chips on a baking sheet. Sprinkle a handful of shredded cheese onto that single layer. Place nachos into oven and bake for just a few minutes, until cheese is almost melted.

    Remove from oven. Place some, not all, of the other ingredients onto that first layer of chips and cheese. Top with another layer of chips, more cheese, and the remaining ingredients.

    Put nachos back in oven and bake until cheese melts. Watch carefully.

    Of course you can use whatever toppings you like, and you can serve with salsa, sour cream, guacamole, hot sauce, or . . . you get the idea.

"It only gets better!" That's how I feel about life, and that's also how I feel about leftover Carnitas Pork! If—and that's a big if—you have any pork that's not eaten at your Taco Bar party, you can use it to make these simple, tasty nachos.

*T*his collection of recipes can set your tailgate party apart from the rest. In the spirit of simplicity, you could prepare everything ahead of time, on your grill at home or in your kitchen, and just heat things up on a small Weber or hibachi onsite. Of course, if you're one of those people who go "all out" with the tailgate gear, go ahead and smoke your ribs and grill your kielbasa in the parking lot—more power to you!

*KIX STORY*: Barbecued ribs. Smoked ribs. Falling-off-the-bone baby back ribs. If you're serving ribs at your shindig, you're going to be popular. You don't have to save your rib eating for a restaurant or barbecue shack. No sir! You, yes you, can make ribs for your next tailgater or backyard get-together. I'm not kidding! I'm giving you two ways to do it right here in this book. The first way is a St. Louis–Style sparerib recipe. The second idea is for Hickory-Smoked Barbecued baby back ribs, one of my all-time favorites.

# ST. LOUIS-STYLE RIBS

**Racks of spareribs**
**Salt**
**Black pepper**
**Onion powder**
**Garlic power**

**Your favorite barbecue or pork rub (see James' Famous Pork "Butt" Rub recipe in this chapter)**
**Straight-Up Barbecue Sauce (see recipe in chapter 6) or your favorite bottled barbecue sauce**

Heat grill to high.

Rinse the ribs under running cold water. Blot them dry with paper towel. On the bone side of the slab, there's a tough membrane covering the bones. Remove this membrane by getting between it and the meat at the wider end of the slab and ripping it off all the way to the narrow end. You may have to start with a sharp knife, and then you should be able to pull it off with your hands.

Coat the ribs liberally with salt, pepper, onion powder, and garlic powder. Put them on the grill meaty side down. Leave the grill open, and stay close by. After about 5 minutes, turn the rack of ribs a quarter turn, still meaty side down. This will make for some nice grill marks.

Turn off the burner that the ribs are on. If you're using charcoal, move the ribs to a side not directly over the hot coals. From here on, only cook on the "off" burner or indirect heat side of the grill.

Turn the ribs over to bone side down and cook for about 1 hour. Brush barbecue sauce over the ribs during the last 15 minutes of baking.

Sprinkle the ribs with your favorite rub. Remove from the grill, and cut the rack into individual ribs. In a large bowl, toss the ribs with more barbecue sauce, and then put them back on the grill for a few minutes. The heat will caramelize the sugar in the sauce and make the ribs nice and crusty.

*KIX TIP:* While St. Louis–Style ribs are typically spareribs, you could use baby back ribs instead; you'll just need more ribs. Each slab of spareribs will typically feed three to four, while an average rack of baby back ribs will only feed about two. Just so you know, back ribs are cut from where the rib meets the spine after the loin is removed. The upper ribs are called baby back ribs, but not because they come from a baby pig. They're called "baby" because they are shorter in relation to the bigger spareribs. Baby back ribs tend to be tender and lean. There's a higher amount of fat in spareribs, which makes them very flavorful if cooked properly. Spareribs are flatter than baby back ribs, which makes browning them easier.

❯ **Makes 3 or 4 servings per rack of spareribs; 2 servings per rack of baby back ribs.**

# HICKORY-SMOKED BARBECUED BABY BACK RIBS

Mesquite or hickory woodchips, soaked in water or other liquid

Racks of baby back ribs

1/4 cup firmly packed brown sugar

1/4 cup paprika

3 tablespoons freshly ground black pepper

4 tablespoons coarse salt

2 teaspoons garlic powder

1 teaspoon cayenne pepper

Vegetable oil

Apple cider vinegar (put some in a spray bottle if you have one)

Barbecue sauce

Soak about 1 cup of woodchips in water (or beer, wine, whiskey, even apple juice) for at least 1 hour before using. Drain and place them in a woodchip smoker box or in a foil pouch (see Kix Tip).

Rinse the ribs. On the bone side of the slab, there's a tough membrane covering the bones. Remove this membrane by getting between it and the meat at the wider end of the slab and ripping it off all the way to the narrow end. You may have to start with a sharp knife, and then you should be able to pull it off with your hands.

*KIX TIP:* You can make a foil smoking pouch with a 12-inch or larger square of foil. Pile a thin layer of soaked and drained wood chips (about 1/2 to 1 cup of chips) right down the middle of the square. Fold the foil into a rectangle with the chips laid flat in the middle of the rectangle. Seal up the ends of the rectangle and then poke a few holes in the pouch.

Combine the sugar, paprika, pepper, salt, garlic powder, and cayenne in a small bowl to make a rub. Brush a thin layer of vegetable oil on the ribs. Apply a generous amount of the rub to both sides of the ribs. Wrap the ribs in foil or plastic wrap and refrigerate for at least 1 hour.

Ribs grill best with wood smoke and by cooking them slowly over low (indirect) heat. Do this by turning up the heat on only one side of the grill and placing the ribs on the opposite side.

If you don't have a smoker, you can still smoke your ribs! You can get woodchips at Home Depot or Wal-Mart or wherever grills are typically sold. Hickory and mesquite chips are great for smoking ribs. If you don't have a woodchip smoker box, you can make a foil smoking pouch (see Kix Tip).

Now it's time to fire up the grill! Place your smoker box or foil smoking pouch directly on top of one of the burners. Turn that burner to high. Close the lid. Wait until you see smoke coming out of the grill, then turn the burner to medium-low and place the ribs on the grate over the burner NOT in use.

Eventually the woodchips will burn out; once they do, continue cooking the ribs without smoke, until they are done. The wood taste will have already permeated the meat, and your ribs will retain the nice smoky flavor.

> *KIX TIP*: How can you tell if your smoked ribs are done? Well, you could be polite, and stick a toothpick between two bones. If it goes in and out of the meat without resistance, they're done. Or you could do it the fun way, and cut the bone on the end off and taste it. Just make sure there is no pink juice anywhere.

Every half hour or so while the ribs are cooking, lift the lid of the grill, and spray a bit of apple cider vinegar directly on the ribs; this will prevent them from drying out.

The ribs should be fully cooked in 4 to 5 hours. About 20 minutes before they're done, spread a thin coat of your favorite barbecue sauce onto the ribs.

Remove the ribs from grill. Let them rest a few minutes before serving. You can cut the rack into individual ribs and pile them high on a platter for serving.

❷ **Makes 2 servings per rack of baby back ribs.**

**Personally I prefer baby back ribs even though there's less meat on them. My dad always said and I agree, "I don't want those ribs with all that meat on 'em!"**

# SMOKED SAUSAGES

*KIX STORY*: We could talk all day about the different styles and techniques of barbecue, but I'll leave that to the Barbecue Kings to cuss and discuss. My idea of great barbecue to fix for family and friends on the home grill or smoker is sausages and ribs.

I like my sausages smoked—dark brown on the outside and juicy on the inside. Of course, this can be tricky because sausages are high in fat. The fat drips can cause flare-ups on the grill, and that fire can mean *burnt*. Nobody likes a burned sausage! You can smoke just about any kind of sausage: bratwursts, chorizo, bangers, and Italian sausage, and even though kielbasa and hot dogs are typically smoked at the factory, they taste even better with a fresh coat of smoke.

**Soaked woodchips (see directions in Hickory-Smoked Barbecued Baby Back Ribs recipe in this chapter)**

**Sausages of your choice**

**Barbecue sauce, grainy mustards, and other condiments, for serving**

Heat the grill (or smoker if you have one) to about 225 degrees, with the burner on one side turned off. Put the sausages on the indirect heat side, meaning the side with the burner turned off. Add soaked woodchips wrapped in a foil smoking pouch (see Kix Tip in this chapter) to the side of the grill with the direct heat, meaning the side with the burner turned on. Close the lid, and let the sausages smoke for 30 or 40 minutes. There's no need to turn the sausages during this time.

Remove the woodchips, and continue cooking the sausages for another 30 to 60 minutes, until the internal temperature is at least 160 degrees.

You can reverse sear the sausages at the very end of the cooking time by moving them over to the direct heat and letting them get hot and a bit crispy.

*KIX TIP*: Please invest in a decent instant-read or digital meat thermometer, and use it. Seriously, thermometers are not that expensive these days, and they're one of the gadgets that you'll end up using often. There are all kinds of thermometers on the market and even special ones made for the grill. Bottom line is, meat is unsafe if not cooked to proper temperature to kill bacteria, and the best way to know if it's at the correct temperature is with a thermometer.

# KIEL-BABAS

*If you haven't done a lot of grilling, kielbasa is a great "starter" food to grill. It's like a hot dog, in that most of the ones you get at the store are already fully or partially cooked, so all you have to do is heat it up. Pop it on the grill, turn it over a few times, get some grill marks on there, and voila! Perfect on a bun with some grilled onions and mustard. You could also baste a little barbecue sauce on 'em while they're grilling.*

*If you want to get a little fancy, you could try this recipe, which puts kielbasa sausage with some of my other grill favorites—peppers, mushrooms, and onions—on a skewer. Food on a stick is perfect for tailgating—no forks or plates to mess with, and you still have a free hand for your favorite beverage.*

**Smoked or fresh kielbasa sausage, as many as you need to feed your crowd**

**Bell peppers, any color, cut into chunks**

**Whole medium mushrooms, wiped clean, cut in half**

**White or red onion, cut into chunks**

**Pineapple chunks, fresh or canned (optional)**

**Metal skewers, or wooden skewers, soaked in water**

**Olive or canola oil**

**Salt**

**Black pepper**

**Any other spices you like, such as crushed red pepper flakes**

If you bought fresh kielbasa sausages, you'll need to precook them before you grill them. If that's the case, the night before your tailgate party, simmer the whole kielbasa sausages in a big pot of water (or beer) for 10 to 15 minutes. Remove the sausages from the water, and set aside to cool. When cooled, cut the sausages into 1- to 2-inch chunks and put in big plastic ziptop bag in fridge overnight. Clean and cut all your vegetables as well and place them in separate bags to chill overnight.

If you bought smoked kielbasa, there is no need to boil it. Just cut the sausages into chunks, and refrigerate them until you're ready to assemble your skewers.

The next day, you can easily transport the sausage and veggies in a cooler to your party place. Heat the grill, and skewer the sausage and veggies, alternating veggies with meat to your liking. Brush with oil and sprinkle with salt, pepper, and any other spices you like.

Place the skewers directly onto grill, basting with more oil if you want. Grill until the veggies and pineapple get a nice char on them.

Now, if you get a hankering for a Kiel-baba and you don't have a grill handy, you can always put them under the broiler, watching them closely, and turning until they're browned and a bit charred on all sides. Once browned to your liking, turn the oven to 425 degrees and let them hang in the oven for another 10 minutes or so.

Whichever way you do it, once they're browned, remove them from the heat and wrap them in foil until ready to serve.

These shish kababs are delicious straight off the skewer. You can dip them in any kind of mustard, barbecue sauce, teriyaki, or whatever sounds good to you.

**❯ Makes 4 servings per 1-pound kielbasa.**

*KIX TIP:* The key is to cut your veggies and your sausage to the same size pieces in order for everything to cook evenly on the grill.

Tailgating is not just about eating; it's about getting fired up for a game or concert or whatever event. It's about good food that goes well with festive drinking.

**KIX TIP:** I know you know this already, but if you're not eating this potato salad warm right after you prepare it, you've got to keep it chilled until you are ready to eat it. Put any leftover salad back into the cooler or fridge immediately. I don't want anybody getting sick at the party!

# SMASHED TATER SALAD

*There are a million ways to make potato salad, but this technique of smashing the potatoes in the bowl makes for a nice texture. The potatoes aren't in chunks, and neither are they completely mashed like mashed potatoes. It's a good in-between place, and if you smash them up in a big Tupperware bowl with a lid, it's easy to transport this side dish to your tailgate party or church picnic.*

**2 pounds small potatoes (the little red ones are good), scrubbed and cut into 1/2-inch pieces**

**2 teaspoons salt, divided**

**1/2 cup yellow or sweet red onion, minced**

**3 hard-boiled eggs, chopped (see Deviled Eggs recipe in chapter 5 for perfectly cooked hard-boiled eggs)**

**1 teaspoon minced garlic**

**3/4 cup mayonnaise**

**1/4 cup Dijon mustard, stone-ground mustard, or regular yellow mustard**

**2 tablespoons fresh lemon juice**

**1 tablespoon brown sugar**

**1/2 teaspoon hot sauce (see Kickin' It Hot Sauce recipe in chapter 6)**

**1/2 teaspoon Worcestershire sauce**

**1 to 2 teaspoons freshly ground black pepper**

Boil the potatoes in enough water to cover with 1 teaspoon of the salt until fork tender, about 10 minutes. Drain and transfer the potatoes to a large mixing bowl.

Mash the potatoes with a hand-held potato masher or sturdy fork. Keep them a little bit lumpy. Mix in the onions, eggs, and garlic.

Mix in 1/2 cup of the mayonnaise along with the mustard, lemon juice, and brown sugar, stirring to dissolve the sugar. Add the rest of the mayonnaise if the mixture seems dry and even more if you want it "wetter." Season with the hot sauce, Worcestershire sauce, pepper, and the remaining salt. Stir well, then taste. Add more salt, lemon juice, mustard, or whatever you think it needs. Yes, it's up to you; this is your potato salad, and these are your decisions to make. Serve right away or chill before serving.

❯ **Makes 6 to 8 servings.**

# GRILLED PEACHES

*You'll want firm, fresh peaches for grilling. It's okay if they're a little soft, but you don't want to put a mushy peach on the grill, as it will disintegrate and be hard to remove. You can bring whole fresh peaches to a tailgate party or summer picnic in the park, and slice them right before you grill them.*

**Sugar, raw, regular, or brown**

**Fresh peaches**

**Vegetable oil or melted butter**

**Balsamic vinegar**

**Fresh mint or basil, for garnish**

Heat the grill.

Pour the sugar onto a small plate, covering plate completely. Wash the peaches and leave skins on. Cut the peaches in half and remove the pits.

Brush the flesh side of each peach half lightly with oil or butter. Dip each peach, flesh side down, in the sugar.

Carefully place each peach, sugared side down, on the hot grill. Grill until marks form and peaches start to release juice, for just a few minutes. Turn over, and grill for another minute or so.

Transfer peaches to a plate, drizzle with a small amount of balsamic vinegar, and place a fresh mint or basil leaf on top of each. These warm, sweet peaches can be picked up and eaten by hand or served on a plate with a fork.

❱ **Makes 1 serving per peach.**

*KIX TIP:* You don't have to fire up the grill to make these peaches. You can always put them on a sturdy baking sheet or broiler pan, and broil them on the top rack of the oven until they start to bubble. Watch them closely so they don't burn. Once they're hot and juicy, turn off the oven and let them hang in there for a few minutes before serving.

# ROASTED CORN

*Corn on the cob is another one of my favorites. I like it roasted in the husk, sheared off the cob and browned in a skillet with butter, even boiled in hot water. It's one of those things that you really can't mess up, which gives you a chance to play around with spices, butters, herbs, and all kinds of fun stuff. Give my ideas a try, and then make up some of your own.*

**Corn on the cob, in the husk**

**Butter or Compound Butters (see recipes)**

**Salt**

**Black pepper**

Soak the corn in the husks in a sink filled with cold water for 30 minutes or so. You can soak it the night before, and then put it in plastic ziptop bags or wrap in foil to transport to your tailgate the next day if you want to. Just keep it in the fridge until you're ready to leave.

Now, here's the hard part (not!). Plop the soaked corn, in the husk, right onto the hot grill. Keep an eye on it, and turn it every few minutes until it's all charred and marked up. Remove it from grill.

Once the corn is cool enough to handle, pull the husks off, smear with butter or one of the Compound Butters, and sprinkle with salt and pepper or whatever seasoning sounds good. Here are some thought starters: cayenne pepper, cumin, chili powder, crushed red pepper flakes . . . you get the idea!

*KIX TIP:* You can remove the husks from your corn first if you want, and lay it "naked" right on the grill. You can also remove the husks, and drop the corn in boiling water and let it cook for 3 to 4 minutes. Remove it from the water, and let it drain for a few minutes before smearing on the butter.

❷ **Makes 1 serving per ear of corn.**

# COMPOUND BUTTER

*Compound butter is as much a technique as a recipe. Step one is to let a stick of unsalted butter come to room temperature. Step two is mixing that softened butter with any number of herbs and spices and other ingredients to make the compound butter. Once you have the butter and the other ingredients mixed together well, roll the butter into a log and wrap it in waxed paper. Freeze the log of butter. Remove the butter from freezer about 30 minutes before you're ready to eat, and slice off thin rounds for serving.*

**Roasted Garlic Butter**
**1 head garlic**
**¹/₂ cup (1 stick) butter, softened**
**Olive oil**

**Pinch of black pepper**
**1 to 2 teaspoons salt**
**1 to 2 teaspoons Herbes de Provence**
**Zest of 1 lemon**

Preheat the oven to 300 degrees.

Cut off the top of the head of garlic, so that you can see the tops of the individual cloves. Place the head on a square of foil. Drizzle olive oil over top, and sprinkle with pepper and pinch of salt. Roast in the oven for 30 to 45 minutes, until the garlic is soft.

*KIX TIP:* A pat of compound butter is perfect on top of a hot steak!

Remove from oven, and let cool for a few minutes. Squeeze the roasted garlic cloves into the softened butter. Mix in the remaining salt, Herbes de Provence, and lemon zest. Roll the butter into log, and wrap in waxed paper. Freeze until ready to use.

❯ **Makes ¹/₂ cup.**

# JALAPEÑO CILANTRO BUTTER

**¹/₂ cup (1 stick) butter, softened**
**2 fresh jalapeño peppers, seeded and minced**

**2 pickled jalapeño peppers, seeded and minced, plus 1 tablespoon of brine from jar**
**¹/₂ cup chopped cilantro**
**Pinch of salt**

Combine the butter, peppers, cilantro, and salt in the bowl of a food processor. Pulse until evenly blended and smooth. (Or place the ingredients in a bowl, and stir with a fork until smooth.) Once mixed, roll into log, and wrap in waxed paper. Freeze until ready to use.

❯ **Makes ¹/₂ cup.**

# OTHER COMPOUND BUTTER IDEAS

Try mixing any of these with $\frac{1}{2}$ cup (1 stick) softened butter:

**A handful of fresh herbs, such as basil,
oregano, thyme, and sage**

**Anchovies**

**Wasabi powder**

**Cheese**

**Any kind of spice or seasoning, such as
cumin and chili powder**

Taste the butter to see if you need to add extra salt.

**KIX STORY:** My longtime friend Chris Waters Dunn was generous enough to share this enchilada casserole recipe with me. It's from his award-winning cookbook *Enchiladas Aztec to Tex-Mex*. Chris was a songwriter (and a darn good one!) before he went off and launched his second career as a chef. He was kind enough to send me a story for this cookbook, and I was so touched by it that I didn't change a word.

There has always been something special about my relationship with Kix. We instantly clicked—both as cowriters and as friends. The first time we got together to write a song, March 20, 1985, we started work on the title, "You Made a Rock of a Rolling Stone," which turned into a hit single for the Oak Ridge Boys.

In January 1986, we wrote "I Still Hear the Music of Nashville," winner of the Nashville Song Challenge. The prize was a trip to Hawaii, where I drove a golf cart around the Ka'anapali Golf Course guarding the beer while Kix (framed by a rainbow, no less) sank several impressive putts.

That same year we wrote "Why Wyoming," recorded by my sister Holly Dunn. I'm very proud to have been part of that song with Kix, and it's one of Holly's favorite recordings.

A couple of years later, we penned "If It Wasn't for the Heartache," recorded by Jill Hollier for the Clint Eastwood movie, *Pink Cadillac*. We went to the Nashville premiere, and I'll never forget the moment we finally heard our tune—Eastwood was at a bar in the men's room flushing a toilet while the chorus played in the background.

Luckily, Kix didn't give up on me. In the mid- to late '90s we wrote several songs for Brooks & Dunn, including the Top 10 single, "Why Would I Say Goodbye." We finished the verses sitting at Kix's kitchen table while his wife, Barbara, was making red beans and rice.

Come to think of it, food and music have always been intertwined in our lives and careers. Over the years we've shared everything from roast pig at a luau on Maui to pimento cheese sandwiches on a tour bus. Nowadays, Kix has gained even more fans "steaking" out steak houses for the Cooking Channel, and I've gained a few inches hanging around and writing about Tex-Mex enchilada joints.

There have been a lot of memorable moments, but what means the most to me is that, throughout it all, Kix has always been the same ol' Kix—bigger than life, a great person, and a true friend.

—CHRIS WATERS DUNN

# PASTEL AZTECA

*Pastel Azteca, which translates as "Aztec cake," is an enchilada casserole composed of alternating layers of corn tortillas, tomato sauce, shredded chicken, poblano chilies, cheese, and crema Mexicana (sour cream). To cook the chicken, use your favorite method of preparation, moisten with broth, cover, and refrigerate until needed. (This recipe is adapted from* Enchiladas Aztec to Tex-Mex *by Cappy Lawton and Chris Waters Dunn.)*

## Sauce

**2 pounds Roma tomatoes**

**3/4 cup water**

**1/2 medium white onion, peeled and roughly chopped**

**2 cloves garlic**

**2 tablespoons vegetable oil**

**Kosher salt, to taste**

## Filling

**6 poblano chilies**

**3 boneless, skinless chicken breast halves (8 ounces each), cooked**

## To assemble

**Vegetable oil, for frying tortillas**

**12 corn tortillas**

**1 tablespoon butter or vegetable oil, for greasing casserole**

**1 1/2 cups crema Mexicana or sour cream**

**1 1/2 firmly packed cups Monterey Jack cheese**

**Chopped tomato, for garnish**

Heat the grill.

To prepare the sauce, place the tomatoes in a saucepan, add the water, cover, and cook over medium-low heat until the tomatoes begin to burst open. Set aside to cool slightly in the cooking liquid.

Using a slotted spoon, transfer the tomatoes to a blender along with the onion and garlic. Blend to a very smooth purée, adding a little tomato cooking liquid as needed to achieve a thick sauce consistency.

Heat the oil in a saucepan over medium heat. Add the tomato purée, and cook until it slightly darkens, for 10 to 15 minutes. Season with salt to taste, cover, and set aside.

To prepare the filling, place the whole chilies directly on the grill grate over hot coals or a gas flame. Turn the chilies until blackened evenly. When chilies are evenly blistered and blackened, remove and place them in a paper bag. Place the paper bag inside a plastic bag, seal, and allow the chilies to steam for several minutes (until cool enough to handle). When cool, remove the skins, stems, veins, and seeds from chilies, and slice into strips. To maintain maximum flavor, chilies should not be rinsed with water.

Preheat the oven to 350 degrees.

Shred the chicken into bite-size pieces, and mix with two-thirds of the poblano strips.

To assemble the casserole, pour the oil to a depth of $\frac{1}{2}$ inch in a heavy skillet and place over medium-high heat. Heat to 300 degrees. Place the tortillas in the oil one at a time, and fry for a few seconds, just long enough to soften. Drain on paper towels.

Butter or oil a shallow, ovenproof baking pan that will accommodate 4 tortillas in a single, slightly overlapping layer, about 8 $\frac{1}{2}$ inches by 12 inches.

Spread a few tablespoons of the tomato sauce on the bottom of the pan.

Place 4 softened tortillas in a single layer on top of the tomato sauce, followed by half of the chicken mixture, one-third of the remaining tomato sauce, $\frac{1}{2}$ cup crema Mexicana, and $\frac{1}{2}$ cup cheese.

Layer with 4 more tortillas, the remaining chicken mixture, $\frac{1}{2}$ of the remaining tomato sauce, $\frac{1}{2}$ cup crema Mexicana, and $\frac{1}{2}$ cup cheese.

Top with the last 4 tortillas and the remaining tomato sauce, crema Mexicana, and cheese. Decorate the top with the reserved poblano strips.

Bake 15 to 20 minutes, until the cheese is melted and the pastel is heated through.

Remove from oven and garnish with the chopped tomato. Loosely cover with aluminum foil, and let rest for a few minutes before serving.

This is a great dish to make ahead and it transports well. You can serve it at room temperature or you can reheat it on a grill or in an oven.

❯ **Makes 6 to 8 servings.**

# TAILGATING BEVERAGE IDEAS

Here's a list of beverages that are perfect for taking with you to any tailgate party or other outdoor gathering. They all make a big batch and can all easily be doubled, plus you can serve these drinks in plastic cups or other nonbreakable outdoor glasses. You can find the recipes for everything on this list in chapter 8: Libations, Cocktails and Beverages.

**Grapefruit-Basil Sangarita:** This sangria/margarita punch goes perfectly with the Taco Bar in this chapter. The fruity, delicious mocktail version is a crowd-pleaser as well.

**Apple Cider:** You won't go wrong bringing this warm cider to a fall football tailgater. It's easy to "spike" for the adults too.

**Bourbon Slushies:** Think hot summer day on the lake or at the beach; this icy drink will cool everybody down. It also pairs well with picnic foods like ribs or grilled kielbasa sausages.

**Southern Tea:** Iced tea, sweet tea, peach tea; take your pick and bring a gallon or two along wherever the party takes you. Lemons, fresh mint, and peach slices can be packed into ziptop plastic bags and packed in the cooler for easy, festive garnishes.

**KIX STORY:** Before I tell you the story of my first Turkey Frying Fiasco, I want to talk about the Thanksgiving holiday itself and how it usually works at my house. My grown children, Molly and Eric, who live on opposite ends of the United States, usually make their way home, and, of course, they're invited to bring their friends along. Then my wife, Barbara, and I also invite various friends and folks who, for one reason or another, don't have anywhere to go or any family to hang out with for that day. There's nothing more fun than a houseful of talking and laughing and cooking commotion. When we all sit down at the table and start passing around the piles of food, I realize how blessed I truly am.

Now, back to that deep fried turkey incident that nearly ended up with a burned-down deck. This was back in the day, before all the fancy turkey fryers came on the market. We wired up the turkey on a coat hanger and used a broomstick to lower it down into that hot oil. Yes, we caught the yard on fire but, heck, ain't it fun to raise a little hell at the holidays? There's really no better way to do it than with a cold turkey on a coat hanger and an overfilled pot of smokin' hot grease!

After learning everything the hard way that first time, I finally figured out how to fry a turkey for real. Step one: go to the local hardware store or Walmart and buy yourself a proper turkey fryer. Step two: follow the directions!

Since my cookbook publisher didn't want to be responsible for folks burning down their houses, I decided to give you an alternative Thanksgiving turkey recipe. This one's pretty fun too. You get to hack out the turkey backbone and crack the breast plate and then brag to everybody about how you spatchcocked the bird!

Besides the Spatchcocked Turkey, I've got some family favorites on this holiday menu. Eat up!

## The Menu

**Spatchcocked Turkey**

**Barbara's Veggie Stuffing**

**Cranberry Orange Sauce**

**Creamed Onions**

**Asparagus Mold**

**Molly's Pumpkin Pie**

# SPATCHCOCKED TURKEY

*Just so you know, "spatchcocking" means flattening out a bird by removing its backbone and cracking its breast plate. It allows everything to cook more evenly and more quickly. It's an easy way to get juicy meat and crispy skin—the perfect bird.*

**1 turkey, thawed, any size you want as long as it fits on a roasting pan or baking sheet that fits in your oven**

**Olive oil**

**Salt**

**Pepper**

**1 tablespoon onion powder, or more**

**1 large yellow or white onion, cut into quarters or rings**

**A handful of fresh thyme or other herbs**

**Juice of 1 to 2 oranges, for basting**

**Softened butter, for basting**

Preheat the oven to 400 degrees.

Use kitchen shears or a cleaver or both to cut out the backbone of the turkey. There are plenty of online videos showing step-by-step directions on how to do this.

After you get the backbone cut out, trim off extra skin and fat, and spread out the bird, breast side up. Press down in the middle of the breast, and push down until the breast plate cracks and your turkey is lying pretty flat.

Drizzle olive oil over the entire turkey. Sprinkle salt, pepper, and onion powder over the entire bird, and gently rub in the spices. Don't be afraid to use plenty of salt and pepper. There isn't an exact amount to use, but you want the whole bird covered with a thin layer of salt and pepper on both sides.

Spread the onion and fresh herbs on a large roasting pan or baking sheet. Lay the turkey, breast side up, on top of the onions and herbs.

Tent foil over the turkey, and bake for 20 minutes. Pull the turkey out after 20 minutes, and brush it with orange juice and dot it with softened butter. Reduce the heat to 350 degrees, and return the turkey to the oven.

Check the turkey every half hour or so, and baste with more orange juice and butter. Cooking time varies depending on size of the bird. A 13- to 14-pound turkey will probably be done in another 1 1/2 hours. A bigger bird will take longer, of course. Use an instant-read thermometer, and check the turkey (pushing thermometer into thickest part of thigh) every so often. You want the temperature to register at least 165 degrees.

*KIX WINE NOTE:* Riesling is the classic pairing with turkey, and it works well. I prefer a dry Riesling, but another favorite of mine is rosé. Fun fact: rosé is actually a red wine that is processed without the grape skins, which is why it's paler than a typical red. Pairing rosé with the turkey gives you something uniquely different than a white wine, and it works beautifully.

Remove the foil tent for last 20 minutes of cooking time so turkey can get nice and brown. Let the turkey rest before carving.

# BARBARA'S VEGGIE STUFFING

*This is one of those recipes that evolved, meaning somebody cut it out of a magazine and sent it to somebody else. And then that person thought it would taste even better if they added this instead of that, and before you know it, it's like a rumor in the grapevine—it turns into something else completely!*

*This is my wife Barb's recent addition to our Thanksgiving spread and it's delicious.*

4 cups water

1 cup wild (or brown) rice, prepared and cooled

1/2 pound cubed bread (white, wheat, or a combination)

1/2 cup (1 stick) butter, plus 2 tablespoons melted butter or reserved fat from turkey

2 cups diced onion

2 cups diced celery

1/4 cup diced mushrooms (optional)

1/4 cup water chestnuts (optional)

1/4 cup diced red bell pepper (optional)

2 cups diced Granny Smith apple

1/4 cup chopped pecans

1/4 cup finely chopped fresh flat-leaf parsley

2 tablespoons finely chopped fresh sage or 1 1/2 teaspoons dried, crumbled sage

2 teaspoons ground cumin

1 teaspoon finely chopped fresh thyme or 1/4 teaspoon dried, crumbled thyme

1 teaspoon salt

1/2 teaspoon black pepper

1 cup dried cranberries

1 to 2 cups vegetable broth or turkey or chicken broth

Prepare the rice ahead of time and spread it out to cool on a baking sheet.

Preheat the oven to 350 degrees.

Spread the bread cubes on a baking sheet or shallow baking pan, and bake about 20 minutes, until dry.

*KIX TIP:* Stuffing can be mixed together without broth and melted butter one day ahead. Cover and chill. Bring to room temperature before adding the broth and melted butter, and proceed with baking.

Melt 1/2 cup of the butter in a large nonstick skillet over medium-high heat. Add all onion, celery, mushrooms, water chestnuts, and bell pepper, and cook, stirring, until softened, for 8 to 10 minutes. Add the apple and pecans, and cook, stirring, until the apples are crisp-tender, about 5 minutes. Stir in the parsley, sage, cumin, thyme, salt, and pepper, and stir for about 2 more minutes. Transfer to a large bowl, and toss with the rice, bread cubes, and dried cranberries.

Pour 1 cup broth and the remaining 2 tablespoons melted butter or turkey fat over the mixture, and mix well. Add more broth, herbs, or salt and pepper, to taste.

Increase oven temperature to 450 degrees and butter a 9 x 13-inch baking dish.

Spread stuffing in the baking dish, and cover tightly with foil. Bake in middle of oven for about 20 minutes. Remove foil, and bake another 10 to 15 minutes, until the top is browned.

❯ **Makes 8 servings.**

# CRANBERRY-ORANGE SAUCE

1 (12-ounce) bag cranberries, rinsed and drained

Enough water to completely cover berries in a large pot

½ cup granulated or raw sugar

½ cup packed brown sugar

1 tablespoon orange zest

¼ cup freshly squeezed orange juice

1 teaspoon cinnamon

¼ teaspoon ground ginger

¼ teaspoon ground cloves

¼ teaspoon ground nutmeg or freshly grated nutmeg

Splash of brandy or cognac

1 cinnamon stick

Place the rinsed cranberries in large pot, and cover with water. Bring to boil. When cranberries start to split and pop, reduce the heat to low, and simmer. Stir in the sugars, orange zest and juice, cinnamon, ground ginger, ground cloves, ground nutmeg, and brandy. Add the cinnamon stick.

Let the sauce simmer for several hours, stirring occasionally. You shouldn't have to add additional liquid unless you prefer a thinner sauce. The sauce is actually cooked and ready to eat after about 15 to 20 minutes, but it gets thicker and better the longer you let it simmer.

❯ Makes 8 to 10 servings.

# ASPARAGUS MOLD

*KIX STORY*: The first time I sat down for Thanksgiving dinner with my in-laws, Barb's mother brought out this weird-looking green and red Jell-o thing with asparagus and olives and nuts in it. I was dreading having to be polite and put a slice on my plate. But I manned up, and, heck, I was glad I did. Believe it or not, this thing tastes good; it's kind of like a relish, so it goes great with turkey and stuffing. If you don't have a real mold pan lying around (and who does?), you can use a Bundt pan or a glass baking dish. Seriously, you ought to try it; I think you'll like it!

3/4 cup sugar

1/2 cup distilled white vinegar

1 cup water

2 tablespoons unflavored gelatin (such as Knox Gelatine)

1/2 cup cold water

1 cup chopped celery

1/2 cup chopped pecans or walnuts (optional)

2 (2-ounce) jars chopped pimientos

1 (16-ounce) can chopped asparagus, drained, or 1 pound fresh asparagus, steamed or boiled with salt until it's soft, then drained and chopped

Juice of 1/2 lemon

2 teaspoons finely minced or grated onion

1/2 cup pimiento-stuffed green olives

1/2 teaspoon salt

Sour Cream Dressing (see recipe)

Mix the sugar, vinegar, and water in a small saucepan, and bring to boil over medium-high heat. Cook for at least 2 minutes. Remove from heat.

Dissolve gelatin in the cold water, and let sit for 5 minutes. Add gelatin to vinegar mixture. Mix in the celery, pecans, pimientos, asparagus, lemon juice, onion, olives, and salt. Pour into 1 1/2-quart mold. Refrigerate until completely set.

To remove from mold, place mold in a bowl of hot water. Invert mold onto serving platter or plate. Slice and serve with Sour Cream Dressing.

❷ **Makes 8 to 10 servings.**

# SOUR CREAM DRESSING

**½ cup mayonnaise**

**½ cup sour cream**

Mix mayonnaise with sour cream.
Drizzle over Asparagus Mold.

# CREAMED ONIONS

*I see you turning up your nose at this one, but I'm telling ya, I love me some creamed onions!*

**8 cups water or chicken broth**

**2 tablespoons salt, plus 3/4 teaspoons, preferably kosher or coarse salt**

**2 to 2 1/2 cups pearl onions, peeled**

**6 tablespoons butter**

**6 tablespoons all-purpose or Wondra flour**

**2 cups whole milk**

**Pepper, to taste**

**1/4 teaspoon nutmeg, ground or freshly grated**

**Fresh herbs or paprika, for garnish**

Bring the water and 2 tablespoons of the salt to a boil, then carefully drop in the peeled onions. Cook until tender. Drain the onions, reserving liquid. Set the onions aside while you make the sauce.

Melt the butter in a saucepan over medium heat. Add the flour, and whisk until the mixture is bubbly and pasty. Slowly add the milk and half of the reserved cooking liquid to the saucepan, stirring constantly. Increase the heat to medium-high, and bring to a boil, whisking frequently. Stir in the remaining 3/4 teaspoon salt and nutmeg, and add pepper, to taste. Reduce heat to low and cook, whisking occasionally, until thickened, for 12 to 15 minutes. Add the onions, and cook another 5 to 10 minutes.

Transfer the mixture to a serving dish. Sprinkle paprika or fresh thyme, sage, parsley, or oregano on top.

❯ **Makes 8 to 10 servings.**

# MOLLY'S PUMPKIN PIE

*My daughter, Molly, is always in charge of the Thanksgiving pumpkin pie; it's a family favorite. You can dress it up with a fancy whipped cream of course.*

**3/4 cup sugar**

**1/2 teaspoon salt**

**1 1/2 teaspoons ground cinnamon**

**1/2 teaspoon ground ginger or 1 teaspoon grated fresh ginger**

**1/4 teaspoon ground cloves**

**2 large eggs**

**1 (15-ounce) can pumpkin purée (not pumpkin pie mix)**

**1 (12-ounce) can evaporated milk**

**1 unbaked Basic Pie Pastry (see Basic Pie Pastry in chapter 8), chilled, plus more pastry if you want to decorate the top of the pie with leaf cutouts**

**Bourbon-Vanilla Whipped Cream (see recipe)**

Preheat the oven to 425 degrees.

Mix sugar, salt, cinnamon, ginger, and cloves in a small bowl.

Beat eggs in a large bowl. Stir in pumpkin and spice mixture. Gradually stir in evaporated milk.

Pour filling into the unbaked pie shell.

Place the pie in center of oven, and bake for 15 minutes. Reduce oven temperature to 350 degrees, and bake for another 40 to 50 minutes, until a knife inserted in middle comes out clean. Let cool for 2 hours on a wire rack, then serve or refrigerate. Serve with Bourbon-Vanilla Whipped Cream if desired.

❯ **Makes 8 servings.**

*KixTip:* You can substitute 2 teaspoons of pumpkin pie spice for the cinnamon, ginger, and cloves.

# BOURBON-VANILLA WHIPPED CREAM

**1 cup heavy whipping cream, cold**

**¹/₂ teaspoon powdered sugar**

**¹/₄ teaspoon vanilla extract**

**1 tablespoon bourbon or spiced rum**

Chill a large mixing bowl along with the beaters from an electric mixer or a whisk in the freezer for at least 15 minutes.

Pour the cream into the chilled bowl, and mix (or whisk) on high until soft peaks form. Sprinkle in the sugar, and continue mixing on medium-high until the peaks are firmer but not completely glossy. Stir in vanilla and bourbon. Keep chilled until ready to serve.

❯ **Makes about 2 cups.**

# CHAPTER 5
# EASY ON THE SIDES

(Kix's favorite, easy-to-make side dishes)

## BREADS AND SPREADS

# AUNT KATTY

Aunt Katty was my grandmother's sister, which officially made her my *great* aunt, not that that makes any difference for this story, but just so you know.

She was a first-grade schoolteacher for thirty years but never had any children of her own and was only married for a short while. She did not suffer fools or much of anything else really. I guess chasing all those kids for all those years had her patience at the end of the road. She was what you might call a "piece of work," but she loved me.

She lived in Shreveport, so I got to go hang with her quite a bit when I was little. I always looked forward to Sundays when she would pick me up after church and take me to Big Chain Cafeteria where I could get whatever I wanted for lunch as long as I ate it all.

I learned some helpful food cleaning tips from my Aunt Katty too. One day at Big Chain, I got a spot of spaghetti sauce on my white Sunday shirt. She was sitting across the table from me and saw it happen. She never missed a beat; she picked up her full glass of water and threw it right at me, the whole glassful—*BAM!* There I was, soaked, in the middle of the restaurant. I didn't move a muscle—I just laughed. I actually loved it when she went off, and I knew she wasn't quite finished on this particular day. Here she came with a cloth napkin and started scrubbing the heck out of that little spot on my shirt. "We'll get it. Don't you worry." Of course I had a glass of water too, so she was dipping that napkin into my glass and scrubbing that tiny spot until it was completely clean.

I think my favorite part of Aunt Katty doing stuff like that was looking around at all the people with their jaws hanging down, wide-eyed, wondering where we got the crazy pills. Grown-ups don't get it, but seven-year-olds will laugh at anything.

Aunt Katty's most prized possession was her house. She left it to me when she passed away, and I gave it to Habitat for Humanity. I pray that whoever's living there now finds half the joy that I did on 827 College Street. I wrote a song one time with the line, "there's a little slice of heaven on 827," and it was the truth.

Aunt Katty loved cooking, and she loved having parties for any and every occasion. She collected dishes and serving pieces for everything from Thanksgiving to St. Patrick's Day, which made me realize it's fun to "dress it up." Whatever you're eating tastes better when you're having fun.

Now, maybe you're wondering why I chose to tell my Aunt Katty's story at the beginning of the chapter on side dishes. Well, here's why: one of my favorite recipes of hers is these little cheesy baked things called Cheese Wafers. I have a handful of recipe cards from her, in her own handwriting, and the Cheese Wafers recipe is one of them. Actually there are Cheese Wafers, Cheese Puffs, and Cheese Butterflies. Each recipe varies slightly, but the general idea is the same: cheese and butter and some seasonings baked up into a tasty little cheesy snack. I love all of them, and the Cheese Wafer recipe I'm sharing in this chapter is like a crispy cheese cracker. It makes a big ol' bunch of them, so it's perfect for when company's coming or you're throwing an impromptu party in the backyard.

*Aunt Katty's Cheese Wafers (page 137)*

# AUNT KATTY'S CHEESE WAFERS

***KIX STORY:*** If you read the opening story of this chapter you were introduced to my Aunt Katty. When I see her handwriting on the small index recipe cards that she gave to Barbara and me over the years, it's hard not to get sentimental. How lucky I was to have her strong presence in my life. I know for sure that she's one of the reasons I love food and entertaining to this day. She certainly knew how to put on a show.

**1 cup (2 sticks) butter, softened (the original recipe called for 2 sticks of oleo, but let's stick with butter)**

**3 cups shredded Cheddar cheese, preferably sharp Cheddar**

**2 cups all-purpose flour**

**1/2 teaspoon salt (or more to taste)**

**1/4 teaspoon garlic salt**

**1/4 teaspoon cayenne pepper**

**2 cups crispy rice cereal (like Rice Krispies)**

Preheat the oven to 350 degrees.

Mix the butter, cheese, flour, salt, garlic salt, cayenne, and cereal together until you can form the mixture into small balls. You might have to use your hands. It's going to be crumbly, yet moist enough to hold together. Form the mixture into small balls, about 1-inch diameter, and space evenly on an ungreased baking sheet. You can flatten the balls with a fork dipped in cold water to keep it from sticking, if you like.

Bake for 13 to 18 minutes, keeping an eye on them the entire time. Depending on your oven they make bake up sooner or take a bit longer. You want them to be solid enough to lift off the pan with a spatula.

Remove from the oven, and let cool for a few minutes on the baking sheet. Then carefully remove the wafers to a rack or waxed paper to cool completely.

These are great by themselves or also good served with jams, spreads, and roasted garlic. This recipe can easily be doubled.

***KIX TIP:*** You can add more cheese to this recipe if you want, or mix it up and use a couple of different kinds of cheese. Just stick with hard cheeses like Cheddar if you're doing that. I also suggest tasting the mixture before you form it into balls, and make sure it has enough salt for your taste. If you want it saltier, I suggest adding 1/4 teaspoon more at a time until you get it the way you want it. Aunt Katty noted on her recipe card that she sometimes uses less cereal or leaves it out altogether. I'm not sure what happens if you do that because I've never wanted to mess with success. I like the original wafer.

❯ **Makes 2 to 3 dozen wafers, depending on size you make.**

# SWEET ROASTED BRUSSELS SPROUTS

*KIX STORY*: Asparagus, bell peppers, corn, and Brussels sprouts are my favorite vegetables overall. I'm especially fond of Brussels sprouts, and it's a bonus that these little cabbages are so nutritious. Somewhere along the way, I ate some roasted sprouts that I just knew had sugar on them, and man, they were delicious! So, we set out to do a little copycatting and came up with this super-simple recipe. It's so simple I'm almost embarrassed to share it. Make these now.

**1 to 2 pounds Brussels sprouts, rinsed, trimmed, and cut in half**

**Olive oil**

**Sugar, granulated or raw**

**Salt**

Preheat the oven to 375 degrees.

Drizzle a large roasting pan or baking sheet with olive oil. Sprinkle sugar on the pan, in a thin layer, but covering the pan completely.

Place the sprouts cut side down on the pan. This may seem like a lot of trouble, and you *could* just toss the Brussels sprouts willy-nilly on the baking sheet, but taking the time to place each one will give you perfectly roasted sprouts.

Bake for 30 to 40 minutes, turning the sprouts over once or twice if you want. They should be dark brown, almost black, when done. Sprinkle a pinch or two of salt on top and serve immediately.

*KIX TIP:* To trim the Brussels sprouts, pull off any dead or discolored leaves, and cut the hard bottom stalk part off. If the sprouts are small, you can leave them whole for roasting, but cutting them in half makes it easier to lay them flat on the roasting pan.

❯ **Makes 4 to 6 servings.**

# DEVILED EGGS

*KIX STORY*: I thought deviled eggs were mainly a Southern tradition until I did my research and found that there are variations of the deviled egg around the world. Recipes date as far back as ancient Rome. Deviled eggs are usually served cold, as an appetizer or side dish, and they are a common holiday and party food, so of course I had to include a recipe for them in this festive cookbook we've got going here.

12 eggs

$1/2$ cup mayonnaise

$1/4$ cup yellow mustard

1 to 2 tablespoons finely minced onion

1 tablespoon vegetable oil

1 tablespoon grated fresh horseradish

$1/2$ teaspoon salt

$1/2$ teaspoon freshly ground black pepper

1 tablespoon sweet paprika, for garnish

1 tablespoon finely chopped chives, for garnish

Place the eggs in a large pot, and cover with water by 2 inches. Place the pan over high heat, and bring to a boil. Let the eggs boil for 10 minutes. Remove from heat, drain the hot water from the pan, and fill it with cold water. Let eggs stand in cold water, changing water as needed to chill the eggs rapidly.

Peel the eggs, and cut in half lengthwise. Remove the cooked yolks, and place in a mixing bowl. Place egg whites on a serving platter. Add the mayonnaise, mustard, onion, oil, horseradish, salt, and pepper to the yolks. Mix well with a whisk, potato masher, or fork. Fill the egg whites with the yolk mixture, distributing it evenly.

Garnish the eggs with paprika, chives, and bits of bell pepper, or whatever sounds good to you. Chill, covered with plastic wrap, for 6 hours.

*KIX TIP*: Ways to spice and flavor deviled eggs are endless. For example, instead of horseradish and onion, you can stir in some diced pickle or relish or go South of the Border with some chopped chipotle pepper and cayenne pepper. You can top them with bacon bits or caviar or sliced jalapeños or . . . endless possibilities.

❯ Makes 12 servings.

# TABBOULEH SALAD

*KIX STORY*: I met my future wife, Barbara, while I was working at my older sister's advertising agency in Maine shortly after I got out of college. Barbara is originally from Boston, but she owned a fabric and yarn store in the town where my sister lived. Her store was also in the same building where another girl I was dating lived. That "other girl" was having a party one night, and Barbara walked in. I thought to myself, *If I could have her, I wouldn't ask for anything else.* I walked up to her and said something really cool like, "Hey, I'm Kix Brooks, what's your name?" I don't know how it happened, but I upgraded that night, and we've been together ever since, despite our culinary differences. I introduced my new bride to deep-frying, and she convinced me that Tabbouleh Salad was actually something you could eat. This is Barb's recipe. Nothing is fried, and it's still delicious.

1 1/4 cups uncooked bulgur wheat

4 cups boiling water

2 bunches parsley, chopped

1 bunch green onions, chopped

1 (15-ounce) can chickpeas, drained

1/2 cup lemon juice

1/3 cup olive oil

Salt and pepper, to taste

Place the wheat in a large bowl. Pour the boiling water over the wheat, and let it sit for at least 2 hours. Drain well, squeezing with your fingers.

While the wheat is soaking in the water, mix the parsley, green onions, chickpeas, lemon juice, oil, salt, and pepper together in a large bowl. When the wheat has absorbed all the water, fluff it with a fork. Stir the chickpea mixture into the wheat. Serve chilled or at room temperature.

❷ **Makes 6 to 8 servings.**

# OVEN "FRIED" FRIES

*KIX STORY*: Meat and potatoes. What else is there really? Ha-ha! I'm just kidding. I like all the green stuff, and I'll never turn down dinner at an outstanding restaurant with maverick chefs who are cooking to impress. But potatoes are comfort food, and I don't know anybody who doesn't like taters in some form or another. We're keeping it pretty straightforward in this book with a couple of themes and variations on the classic fry. Actually, we're double-frying the regular fries (see Classic Fried Fries recipe in chapter 2) and then giving you a great oven-fried alternative for either regular or sweet potatoes. I'm betting the grown-ups will eat just as many of these as the kids do.

## Potatoes

**2 pounds potatoes, Yukon Golds, russets, or sweet potatoes (4 to 5 potatoes)**
**Olive oil or vegetable oil**
**Salt**
**Pepper**

**Other seasonings, such as crushed red pepper flakes, ground cumin, chili powder, onion powder, garlic powder, or dried oregano . . . get creative!**
**Fresh rosemary, chopped (optional)**
**Sautéed Minced Garlic (optional)**
**1 to 2 tablespoons olive oil**
**3 garlic cloves, minced**

Preheat the oven to 425 to 450 degrees.

To prepare the potatoes, fill a large bowl or pot with ice water. Wash the potatoes and slice, leaving the peel on. You can slice them thin or thick, whatever you prefer. The thinner they are, the faster they'll cook and the crispier they'll be. Drop the potato slices into the ice water, and let them sit for 15 to 30 minutes.

Remove the potatoes from the ice water, and pat them dry with paper towels. Spread them in a single layer on a heavy baking sheet. Drizzle generously with oil, and sprinkle with salt, pepper, and whatever other seasonings you want to add.

Bake for 25 to 35 minutes, flipping the potatoes over at least once to ensure even baking.

To prepare the optional Sautéed Minced Garlic, during the last 10 minutes of baking time, heat a small saucepan over medium heat. Add the oil and garlic. Cook, stirring frequently, until slightly brown. Be careful not to burn the garlic.

When the fries are done, remove from the oven, sprinkle again with salt and pepper, and spoon the warm garlic on top, if using. Toss to coat. Toss the fries with fresh rosemary, if using, just before serving.

*KIX TIP*: Don't ask me why, but soaking the sliced potatoes in the ice water helps them bake up nice and crisp, so don't skip the cold dunk.

❯ **Makes 4 to 5 servings.**

*KIX STORY*: I talk about some of my heroes in this book—my father, my grandfather, my wife, my kids, my great Aunt Katty—all of them inspirational people who have helped make me who I am.

At some point in my life, I realized that I wanted to dig deep inside myself to figure out what motivates me and what I'm all about. When I get down to the nitty-gritty, of course, I'm far from perfect, just like 99 percent of the population. I've vowed to cut off the nasty edges and whittle away at my imperfections until the end of my days; you might say I'm a "work in progress." Because of the way I was brought up and the influence of some of those heroes I just mentioned, my own motivator has always been a higher power. I've always had a strong relationship with God and considered that relationship to be very much a part of my life.

None of us knows what God is exactly, but I do feel like he's a power outside and inside of me. He's certainly a spirit that I can't deceive and someone who has always made me aware of the fact that I'm not getting away with anything. God is my ever-present conscience. This higher power that I'm talking about helps me achieve spiritual success, the greatest challenge of all. And you thought we were just gonna bake some biscuits. Well, we are.

*Jalapeño-Corn Muffins*
*(page 149)*

# ANGEL BISCUITS

*KIX STORY*: These are called Angel Biscuits, which I guess is what got me off on a preaching tangent there for a minute anyway. You have two choices in how you make these: a more traditional way, which will give you a typical biscuit texture, or a slightly unordinary way, which will give you more of a yeast roll texture. Both ways are delicious and freeze well. Make a double batch, put the extra in the freezer, and bring them out when you don't have time to bake but are in the mood for Sunday dinner with your best buddies.

1 (1/4-ounce) package active dry yeast (Fleischmann's Rapid Rise is a great choice)

1/4 cup warm water

5 cups all-purpose flour

7 1/2 teaspoons baking powder

2 teaspoons salt

1 cup regular or butter-flavored shortening (Crisco is a great choice)

1 1/4 to 1 1/2 cups buttermilk, room temperature

1/4 cup sugar

Melted butter

Preheat the oven to 400 degrees.

Dissolve the yeast in the warm water. (The water should be warm on your wrist but not hot enough to burn, 105 to 110 degrees.) Sift together the flour, baking powder, and salt in a large mixing bowl. Cut in the shortening with a pastry cutter or two knives until the mixture is crumbly.

Blend together 1 1/4 cups of the milk with the sugar and yeast mixture. Stir into flour mixture, and blend well. If necessary add more milk to make a soft dough.

*KIX TIP*: This may sound a little strange, but my dad liked his biscuits really crunchy, as I think a lot of folks do. To get these biscuits to turn out crunchy, you need to form or cut them into smaller pieces, and put them close together on the baking sheet. Brush them with melted butter like the recipe calls for or with melted bacon drippings or shortening for even more crispiness. Near the end of the baking time, move them to the top rack of the oven, and broil them for a few minutes to get them extra-brown and crunchy on top. Dad called crunchy biscuits "hickory nuts," and as a kid I loved them made that way. Honestly, "hickory nuts" are still my favorite biscuits, and they're perfect with jam or preserves, such as the Tipsy Fig Preserves, Molasses Apple Butter, and Lemony Tomato Jam recipes in this chapter.

Turn the dough onto a lightly floured surface, and knead gently for 30 seconds. Divide the dough in half, and roll out each half to $1/2$- to 1-inch thick. Cut out biscuits with a biscuit cutter, and place on an ungreased baking sheet. Brush the tops with melted butter right before baking. For regular biscuit texture and flavor, bake immediately for 15 to 20 minutes, or until golden brown. For yeast roll flavor and texture, return the dough to the bowl after kneading, cover the bowl with a tea towel, and let the dough rise in a warm place for 1 hour. Then roll out, cut, and bake as for biscuits.

❯ **Makes about 12 biscuits depending on size.**

*KIX TIP:* If you don't have buttermilk on hand, you can make some by stirring 1 tablespoon white vinegar into 1 cup of whole milk and letting it sit for 5 minutes or so.

# JALAPEÑO-CORN MUFFINS

*These muffins are so sweet and moist that even spicy-food haters will love them! If you left the jalapeño pepper slice off the top, no one would even know there was a hot pepper in there. The secret ingredient is the pumpkin. You don't really taste it, but it makes these muffins very moist.*

**3 tablespoons butter, melted**

**1/3 cup canned pumpkin purée**

**1/4 cup honey**

**1/4 cup raw or regular sugar**

**1 egg**

**1/2 teaspoon salt**

**1/2 teaspoon baking soda**

**2 pickled (or fresh) jalapeño peppers, 1 minced and 1 sliced**

**1 cup buttermilk or regular milk**

**1 cup cornmeal, white or yellow**

**1/3 cup whole wheat flour**

**1/3 cup oat flour**

**1/3 cup all-purpose flour (you can use any combination of flours as long as the total is 1 cup)**

Preheat the oven to 350 degrees. Butter a 12-cup muffin tin.

In large mixing bowl whisk together the melted butter, pumpkin, honey, sugar, and egg. Stir in the salt, baking soda, and minced jalapeño. Stir in the milk. Stir in the cornmeal and flours until combined.

Pour the batter in the muffin tin. Top each muffin with a thin slice of jalapeño. Bake 18 to 22 minutes, until nicely browned and done in the middle. Serve immediately or let cool and freeze.

❍ **Makes 12 muffins.**

*KIX TIP:* These muffins are great with chili, stew, jambalaya, and gumbo. They're also good for breakfast the next day, slathered with some Molasses Apple Butter or any of the other spreads and butters in this chapter.

# PIMENTO CHEESE—TWO WAYS

**KIX STORY:** I usually have a plastic container of pimento cheese in the fridge on my tour bus, and more likely than not it was made by my dear friend Laura Stroud. When I asked Laura for her recipe so that I could include it in this book, she panicked. She told me she just wings it and doesn't really have a recipe. I told her that was fine and that she could just tell me the ingredients and my cookbook fairies would figure out how much of whatever. Being the high achiever that she is though, she made a new batch, measured everything out, and sent me the full recipe. I call it Laura's Wingin' It Pimento Cheese. I've also included another version of this classic spread just for fun.

*Pimento cheese has been called "The Caviar of the South." The basic ingredients are sharp Cheddar cheese, sometimes processed cheese, along with mayonnaise and pimientos. You can spice it up with hot sauce, paprika, jalapeño peppers, or even dill pickles.*

## LAURA'S WINGIN' IT PIMENTO CHEESE

**8 ounces Vermont sharp white Cheddar cheese**

**8 ounces sharp Cheddar cheese**

**1 (2-ounce) jar pimientos, drained**

**Mayonnaise, to taste**

**Small pinch of cayenne pepper (optional)**

The only time-consuming task in making this recipe is dicing the cheese into small cube-like chunks. You could grate it, but it's much better in little square chunks that are less likely to clump up. Once the cheese is diced, place it in a bowl, and add the pimientos. Stir in the mayonnaise to taste. You can add a little or a lot, depending on how you like it. Add the cayenne, if using. Make a sandwich, serve with crackers or veggies, or just eat it with a spoon. Oh yeah!

❯ **Makes 6 to 8 servings.**

# SOUTHERN-STYLE PIMENTO CHEESE

1 (5-ounce) jar sharp pasteurized processed cheese (like Old English Cheese), softened

1 (3-ounce) package cream cheese, softened

1 tablespoon sugar

1/4 teaspoon salt

2 teaspoons lemon juice

1 (2-ounce) jar pimientos, drained and chopped

About 1/2 cup shredded Cheddar cheese, mild, medium, or sharp

In a small bowl, blend softened cheeses together, then add the sugar, salt, lemon juice, pimientos, and shredded cheese. Mix well. Seriously, it's that easy!

❍ **Makes 4 to 6 servings.**

# TOMATO-JALAPEÑO-GARLIC SCHMEAR

*This tasty, spicy spread is great on crackers or as a sandwich condiment or even spread on top of eggs, steaks, or chicken. If you're inside on a rainy weekend day, put a big pan of this in the oven to roast up nice and slow, and honestly, you can't make too much of it, so go big. You can use Roma, cherry, homegrown, or any type of tomato you like. You can even mix it up and use different kinds together.*

**Several tomatoes**

**A handful of jalapeño peppers or your favorite hot peppers, cut in half and seeded**

**Olive oil**

**Salt**

**Pepper**

**1 head garlic, with top trimmed for roasting**

Preheat the oven to 225 degrees.

Cut the tomatoes in half or in quarters if you're using full-size tomatoes. Spread them and jalapeños evenly on a large baking sheet. Drizzle with olive oil, and sprinkle with salt and pepper. Place the head of garlic on a piece of foil, drizzle with olive oil, and sprinkle with a pinch of salt. Wrap the garlic completely in the foil.

Place the baking sheet and wrapped garlic in oven. Check the garlic after 45 minutes or so, and remove from the oven when soft. Set aside.

Continue slow roasting the tomatoes and peppers until the tomatoes start to dry out. You want them very brown but not completely dried. This will probably take a few hours depending on your oven.

Remove from the oven. Squeeze the pulp from the garlic head into the middle of the tomatoes and peppers. Add another drizzle or two of olive oil and maybe some more salt and pepper. With a knife or fork, smash the whole mess together. Taste. It should taste sweet and a bit spicy. Season with more oil, salt, and pepper to taste. Store in the fridge for up to a week.

*KIX TIP:* Slow roasting brings out the sweetness of the tomatoes and mellows out the peppers. A large baking sheet full of tomatoes and peppers will end up making only about 1/2 to 1 cup of spread, so use the biggest pan you have.

❯ **Makes 1/2 to 1 cup.**

# LEMONY TOMATO JAM

*KIX STORY*: I credit a lot of my grounding to spending summers with my grandparents in Marion, Louisiana. When the population of a town is south of a thousand, there aren't a lot of secrets about who you are, and there's not a lot of social climbing to succumb to. Instead, there are a lot of fish to be caught and a lot of Gin Rummy to be played; there's after-dinner church on Sunday and always plenty of fresh okra and tomatoes in the garden.

When the sun is right and the crop is abundant, turn those extra tomatoes into a delicious, savory-sweet jam. This recipe is perfect for tomatoes that are past their prime and turning soft.

**3 pounds fully ripe tomatoes**
**1 lemon, very thinly sliced**

**1 (1 3/4-ounce) package powdered fruit pectin**
**4 cups sugar**

Cut a small X in the bottom of each tomato while bringing a large pot of water to boil. When the water is boiling, gently slide the tomatoes into the water. Boil for 3 minutes. Immediately remove the tomatoes to a big bowl of ice water, and let them cool for 1 minute. Slip the skins off the tomatoes. You can do this while they're floating in the ice water. Once peeled, remove the tomatoes from the water, and quarter them, removing most of the seeds. If you don't want to bother removing the seeds, you don't have to!

Put the tomatoes in a large, heavy pot. Bring them to a boil over medium-high heat, then reduce the heat to low, and simmer for 10 minutes, uncovered, stirring frequently.

Remove from the heat and measure the tomato pulp. You should have at least 3 cups.

Return the pulp to the pan. Add the lemon slices and pectin. Bring to a full boil over medium-high heat, stirring constantly. Add the sugar, and boil rapidly for 3 minutes.

Remove from the heat, and let cool for 5 minutes, stirring often. Put into containers, and store in fridge for up to several weeks.

❯ **Makes 2 pints.**

# TIPSY FIG PRESERVES

*KIX STORY*: On those summer afternoons when I was staying with my grandparents as a young boy, if my grandfather didn't take me fishing, we would head to the garden late in the day. Fresh was king in the country. I can't say I remember doing a lot of weed pulling, but I do remember gathering whatever looked good and fresh for upcoming meals. There were always tomatoes in the summer; we'd have fresh tomatoes with every meal. And then there was—you name it: beans, greens, okra, squash. Oh, and the roses. No, not to eat. I'll tell ya right now, my grandfather wasn't a sissy, but he loved his roses, and that's always stuck with me.

As we'd make our way out of the garden and back to the house, we'd pass a fig tree. I can remember it like yesterday: my grandfather opening his brown bone Case knife, reaching up to carefully cut the stem off a ripe fig so it wouldn't break open, and handing it down to me. There is almost no sweeter natural taste on earth than a ripe fig fresh off the tree. Those figs of my memory would be picked for preserving and put up for later.

If you've never tried making a jam or a preserve, now's the time. You don't have to process any jars and "put up" anything in the cellar; you can make this and store it in the fridge. Trust me, it won't last long anyway. Spread some of this on an Angel Biscuit or one of Aunt Katty's Cheese Wafers . . . oh yeah!

**4 pounds ripe fresh figs, stemmed, cut into 1/2-inch pieces (about 9 cups)**

**3 tablespoons lemon peel, yellow part only, cut into matchstick-size strips**

**4 cups sugar**

**1/2 cup brandy**

**1/2 teaspoon coarse salt**

Combine the figs, lemon peel, sugar, brandy, and salt in a large, heavy, deep saucepan. Let sit at room temperature for 1 hour, stirring occasionally.

Bring mixture to boil over medium-high heat, stirring until the sugar dissolves. Reduce the heat to medium, and continue boiling until the mixture thickens and is reduced to about 6 cups, for 30 to 35 minutes. Stir frequently, and occasionally mash with potato masher. Remove from heat, and let cool slightly.

Ladle the mixture into containers, and store in fridge for up to several weeks.

❷ **Makes 3 pints.**

# CREAMY HONEY BUTTER WITH ORANGE ZEST

*This is another super-simple recipe that stands out any time you're serving freshly baked bread, especially the Angel Biscuits and Jalapeño-Corn Muffins featured in this chapter.*

**½ cup butter, softened**
**½ cup honey**

**Finely grated zest from 1 to 2 oranges**

Place the butter, honey, and orange zest in a small mixing bowl. Using an electric mixer, beat until creamy. (You could use a whisk if you need to work out your arm muscles!) This recipe can be doubled if you're expecting a lot of company. It keeps in the fridge for up to a month.

❯ **Makes 1 cup.**

# MOLASSES APPLE BUTTER

*KIX STORY*: Sometimes part of the fun of food is digging into the history of an ingredient or a recipe. For example, in working on this recipe for apple butter, I learned that it dates back to the Middle Ages. The monasteries of that time often had orchards, and making apple butter was a perfect way to preserve part of their fruit production. Apple butter was also popular in colonial America. There's no actual dairy butter in apple butter, but the final product has the consistency of spreadable butter and is often spread on bread just like butter would be. You can use a variety of apples to make this butter or just use your favorite crisp apple.

1 cup granulated or raw sugar

1 cup packed brown sugar

2 teaspoons ground cinnamon

¼ teaspoon salt

6 pounds of apples, peeled, cored, and sliced (about 12 apples)

1 tablespoon molasses

1 cinnamon stick

Whisk together the sugars, ground cinnamon, and salt in a medium bowl. Layer about one-third of the apples into a slow cooker, and sprinkle about one-third of the sugar mixture on top of the apples. Continue to layer the apples and sugar mixture until none remains. Add the cinnamon stick, and drizzle the molasses on top. Cook on low for 10 hours or high for 4 to 5 hours. Stir occasionally.

*KIX TIP*: Take my advice and put this stuff out on the table at every meal and, for sure, at any get-together. It's delicious on toast, biscuits, corn muffins, and crackers or just straight out of the jar! Put a dab on a piece of your favorite cheese, and see how you like that too.

At the end of the cooking time, remove the cinnamon stick for the apple mixture. Use an immersion blender to purée the apple butter until smooth, or purée in batches in a food processor or blender. If you want a thicker butter, you can return the mixture to the slow cooker and cook on low for another couple hours.

Let cool completely, then store in a container in the fridge for up to 2 weeks or freeze for up to 2 months.

❯ Makes about 2 cups.

# CHAPTER 6
# A LITTLE KICK
(rubs, sauces, condiments . . . to make it all better)

# SWEET

*S*ometimes all it takes to kick a dish up a notch or two is a dash of some kind of special sauce or a pinch of seasoning. This chapter is focused on sauces, condiments, and spices that can elevate your food to that next level.

Life itself is kind of like that too; we all have those special people in our lives who bring the "flavor" up a notch or two. One of those special people for me was my grandmother on my dad's side. Edna was her name, and she was a first-grade schoolteacher. Nicknamed "Sweet," she moved in right after my mother died when I was four years old.

I swear *The Andy Griffith Show* was an exact replica of our nuclear family back then. Sweet was built exactly like Aunt Bee, and my dad talked with the same small-town sensibility as Andy Griffith; he even looked like Andy. Of course I starred as little Opie. I'm thankful to whoever dreamed up that scenario for the 1950s television show because it made our situation seem normal. We definitely didn't have the *Leave it to Beaver* household.

As a child, I was very much a monkey on a string. My grandmother taught me how to read and write before I started first grade. She would take me "on tour" to see her friends and bring along props. I would draw and paint pictures with watercolors, Sweet would call out sentences for me to write, and everyone would be amazed. And to think Mozart was doing *Mozart* at that age—good grief!

Sweet drove a 1957 Dodge that she, my sister, and I would all pile into to visit my other grandparents. After forty-five minutes on the road, Sweet would pull over on the side of the highway and take a nap in the car. My sister and I would play in the ditch, throwing rocks at one another while she slept. After she finished her snooze, we'd load up the car and continue on down the road. Those were simpler times for sure.

Sweet was extremely overweight and had diabetes. Sadly, she had a stroke and died when I was seven or eight years old. It was sort of a double whammy, having lost my mom only a few years before. I admit, having two major female figures yanked out from under me at such a young age was hard to digest. I think Sweet might have been the harder blow simply because I was old enough for it to really hurt.

The majority of my self-confidence comes from the love and attention I received from the women in my life. I may have lost my mom and grandma Sweet, but I still had my other grandmother, my aunts, and my sister, and you might say they went slightly overboard to make sure I always had an arm around me. I was surrounded by strong, smart, good women in my life who went out of their way to make sure I wasn't deprived of nurturing. I feel so blessed to have lived my life with so much love and with so many what you might call "spice" or "flavor" or "colorful" characters such as my Aunt Katty, who I talked about in chapter 5, and my grandmother Sweet.

Now, go on and let a little spice into your cooking life; try the recipes in this chapter and "kick" things up a notch!

*Kickin' It Hot Sauce*
*(page 166)*

# KB'S SHREVEPORT SHAKE SEASONING

*Make up a jar of this Cajun-inspired seasoning to have on hand to use anytime a recipe calls for a Cajun or Creole spice or rub. As with just about any spice or rub mix, you can adjust the seasonings to suit your own taste.*

**2 tablespoons sweet Hungarian or Spanish paprika**

**1 tablespoon dried basil**

**1 tablespoon dried thyme**

**1 teaspoon garlic powder**

**1 teaspoon onion powder**

**1/2 teaspoon freshly ground black pepper**

**1/4 teaspoon cayenne pepper**

In a small bowl mix the paprika, basil, thyme, garlic powder, onion powder, pepper, and cayenne. Transfer to a glass jar or other container with a tightly fitting lid. Store in a cool, dark place for up to three months.

❯ **Makes about 1/3 cup seasoning.**

*KIX TIP:* You can double or triple this recipe and share it with your friends.

# KICKIN' IT HOT SAUCE

*KIX STORY*: I know, I know, you're probably thinking, *Why bother with making hot sauce when there are so many great ones already bottled up and ready to buy at the store?* I hear you, but there's something satisfying about making something from scratch every once in awhile. It only takes a handful of ingredients, and hot sauce is actually a simple thing to make at home.

If you're lucky enough to live in an area of the country with a long, hot growing season and you have a garden full of peppers anyway, why not turn some into sauce? You can use a mix of jalapeño, habanero, serrano, or whatever hot peppers you prefer.

**1 pound whole hot peppers, rinsed**
**1/2 onion, chopped**
**Several cloves of garlic, peeled**

**1/2 to 1 cup distilled white vinegar**
**1/2 to 1 cup water**
**2 tablespoons salt**

Preheat the oven to 400 degrees.

Place the peppers, onion, and garlic on a baking sheet, and roast in oven until the peppers are blistered and well browned.

*KIX TIP*: Unlike store-bought, bottled hot sauce, this homemade sauce must be kept in the refrigerator.

Remove the baking sheet from oven, and pull the stems off the peppers. Don't worry about the seeds; you can just leave them in. Place the peppers, onions, and garlic in a big pot; then pour 1/2 cup vinegar and 1/2 cup water over them. If the vegetables are not covered, add more vinegar and water until the vegetables are just covered. Add the salt.

Bring the mixture to a boil over medium-high heat. Reduce the heat to low, and simmer for at least 15 minutes. Turn off the heat, cover the pot, and let the mixture steep until completely cool. Transfer the mixture to a blender or food processor, and process until well blended.

Pour or press the mixture through a fine mesh sieve or strainer. Pour or ladle the sauce into jars or other containers with lids, and store in refrigerator. This will keep for up to a month as long as it's kept in the fridge.

❍ **Makes 1 1/2 to 3 cups.**

# MAKE-YOUR-OWN FISH DIP (TARTAR SAUCE)

***KIX STORY***: Since there are several fish and shrimp recipes in this book, I figured it might be nice to include a recipe for one of the most classic condiments. I'm calling this a dip, but it's got a mayonnaise-tartar sauce base. Once you realize how easy it is to make your own tartar sauce, you may never buy a premade tartar sauce again. Don't be afraid to play around with the spices or amounts either; tweak and taste as you go, and make this dip to your liking.

1 ¼ cups mayonnaise

¼ cup Dijon mustard

¼ cup vegetable oil

¼ cup ketchup

2 tablespoons cider vinegar

1 tablespoon Creole Barbecue Spice (see recipe in this chapter)

1 tablespoon minced onion

1 tablespoon chopped parsley

1 tablespoon lemon juice

1 tablespoon grated fresh horseradish

1 tablespoon dill pickle juice

1 teaspoon hot sauce, more or less to taste

½ teaspoon salt

½ teaspoon freshly ground black pepper

1 tablespoon finely chopped dill pickle

1 tablespoon finely chopped capers (optional)

Place the mayonnaise, mustard, oil, ketchup, vinegar, Creole Barbecue Spice, onion, parsley, lemon juice, horseradish, pickle juice, hot sauce, salt, and pepper in a food processor. Process for about 30 seconds until blended. Scrape down sides of bowl, and process for 15 more seconds. Transfer to a storage container with a lid, and stir in the dill pickle and capers.

Cover and chill in refrigerator for a few hours prior to serving. This will keep in the fridge for up to a week.

❯ Makes about 2 cups.

# STRAIGHT-UP BARBECUE SAUCE

*What I like about this homemade barbecue sauce is that it's super easy to make, and you don't have to cook it. This recipe makes a little over 2 cups, so double it if you think you'll need more sauce than that. This sauce would be great on any recipe calling for barbecue sauce; I especially like it with the ribs recipes in chapter 4.*

**½ cup yellow onion, finely chopped**

**2 cups ketchup**

**¼ cup light corn syrup or Steen's Cane Syrup**

**¼ cup dry red wine**

**1 tablespoon brown sugar**

**½ tablespoon minced garlic**

**½ teaspoon salt**

**¼ teaspoon cayenne pepper, or more to taste**

**1 tablespoon fresh lemon juice**

**1 tablespoon whole-grain mustard, preferably spicy**

**½ tablespoon Worcestershire sauce**

**Dash of hot pepper sauce, or more to taste**

Combine the onion, ketchup, corn syrup, wine, brown sugar, garlic, salt, cayenne, lemon juice, mustard, Worcestershire sauce, and hot pepper sauce in a large mixing bowl. Stir to mix well. Use right away or store in an airtight container in the refrigerator for up to three days.

❯ **Makes about 2 ½ cups.**

# CREOLE BARBECUE SPICE

*This spice mixture is different from KB's Shreveport Shake Seasoning (also in this chapter), even though it has some of the same ingredients. The smoked paprika, cinnamon, and cloves give this blend a deeper, more complex barbecue nature. Rub it on any meat, poultry, or wild game before grilling, or sprinkle it on any vegetable or side dish that you want to have a barbecue flavor.*

2 tablespoons sweet paprika

2 tablespoons dried oregano

2 tablespoons onion powder

2 tablespoons salt

1 tablespoon smoked paprika

1 tablespoon dried chipotle powder

1 tablespoon dried thyme

1 tablespoon garlic powder

1 teaspoon cracked black pepper

1 teaspoon dried parsley

1/2 teaspoon cayenne pepper or crushed red pepper flakes, more or less, depending on desired level of heat

1/4 teaspoon ground cinnamon

1/4 teaspoon ground cloves

Combine all ingredients in a mixing bowl, and stir until evenly distributed and well combined. Store in a tightly sealed container in a cool, dry place.

❷ **Makes about 3/4 cup.**

# STEAK SAUCES

*KIX STORY*: Earlier in this book (chapter 2: Cook Out!), I mentioned things I had learned while hosting *Steak Out with Kix Brooks* on the Cooking Channel, those being how important it is to start with quality meat and then storing that meat in the refrigerator for a few days to allow the enzymes to break down and release flavor.

Another key thing I observed on that show was how the real chefs earn their money with their sauces. I'm talking roasting bones and deglazing with wine and cooking things down until the most flavor is brought out. Those "cats" really know what they're doing, and I can't begin to replicate it. What I can do, though, is give you a basic introduction to making a demi-glace, a sauce that is a base for many other fine sauces.

Now don't panic; we're going to cheat a little bit and bypass all that bone roasting by using a store-bought beef broth. If you screw this up, so what? You can either try again, or when you get the hankering for a perfectly prepared steak with a perfectly prepared steak sauce, you can go out to your favorite steak house! Ha! I think you can do this though.

# DEMI-GLACE AT HOME

1 bay leaf

1 teaspoon dried thyme

6 fresh parsley sprigs

10 whole peppercorns

2 tablespoons clarified butter (see Kix Tip)

½ cup chopped onions

¼ cup chopped celery

¼ cup chopped carrots

¼ cup all-purpose flour

5 cups low-sodium or no-salt beef broth

Salt, to taste

Place the bay leaf, thyme, parsley sprigs, and peppercorns onto a square of cheesecloth, and tie it up into a bundle with twine.

Heat the butter in a heavy pot over medium heat. Add the onions, celery, and carrots. Sauté for a couple of minutes, until the onion is partially translucent.

Slowly stir in the flour to form a paste. Cook for about 3 minutes, stirring frequently, until the flour is lightly browned.

Whisk in about 3 cups of the broth. Bring to a boil; then reduce the heat to low and simmer. Add the bundle of herbs, and cook until sauce is reduced by about one-third.

Remove the pan from the heat, and pull out the herb bundle. Carefully pour the sauce through a wire mesh strainer lined with cheesecloth. Return the sauce and herb bundle to the pan, and stir in the remaining 2 cups of broth. Bring to a boil over medium heat, then reduce the heat to low, and simmer until the sauce is reduced by half, for about 50 minutes.

Remove and discard the herb bundle. Strain the sauce again through a wire mesh strainer and a fresh piece of cheesecloth. You can add salt now or wait until you use the Demi-Glace in another sauce recipe.

Put into a covered container, and keep in the fridge for a couple of weeks, or freeze for up to several months.

❯ **Makes about 1 pint.**

*KIX TIP:* Clarified butter. You can clarify as much butter as you want. Just make sure to use unsalted butter. The reason for using clarified butter instead of regular butter to make the Demi-Glace is that clarified butter can stand being cooked longer than regular butter. Clarifying butter removes the milk solids, which are what cause butter to burn. It's nice to have clarified butter on hand for other things, too, such as scrambling eggs, frying vegetables, or stirring into cooked rice.

Heat whatever amount of butter you want in heavy saucepan over very low heat until the butter is melted. Let it simmer gently until the foam rises to the top. Remove from the heat, and skim off the foam with a spoon. Get as much as you can, but don't stress if you can't get every bit of the foam out.

Line a mesh strainer with a few layers of cheesecloth, and set the strainer over a heatproof container. Carefully pour the warm butter through the strainer into the container, leaving behind any solids from the bottom of the pan. Clarified butter will keep for three to six months in the refrigerator.

# BRANDY CREAM MUSTARD SAUCE

1 tablespoon olive or vegetable oil

2 shallots, finely chopped

1/2 cup brandy

1/2 cup low-sodium beef broth

2 tablespoons Dijon mustard

2 teaspoons fresh thyme leaves

1/2 cup heavy cream

1 tablespoon honey (optional)

Salt

Freshly ground black pepper

Dash of cayenne pepper (optional)

Heat the oil in a large cast-iron skillet or other heavy skillet over medium-high heat. Add the shallots, and cook, stirring, until tender, for 4 to 5 minutes. Remove the pan from the heat, and stir in brandy. Be careful; the brandy might flame up a bit.

Return the pan to heat, and add broth, mustard, and thyme; stir to blend. Add the cream and honey, if using. Reduce the heat to low, and simmer until the sauce is slightly thickened, for 4 to 5 minutes. Remove from the heat, and season with salt, pepper, and cayenne, if using.

❷ **Makes about 1 to 1 1/2 cups.**

*KIX TIP*: This Brandy Cream Mustard Sauce is great with steaks but also good with chicken. You could add crushed green peppercorns to this sauce at the end for variety.

# CHAPTER 7
# SWEETS AND INDULGENCES

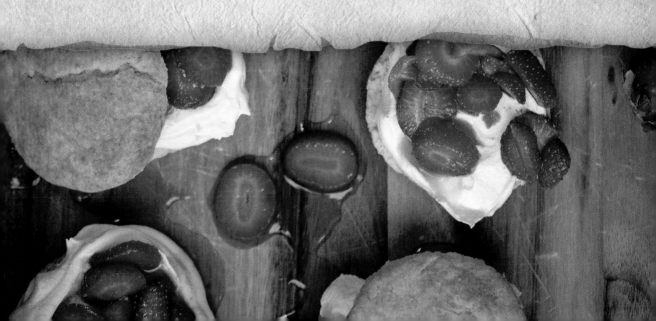

# COMMANDER'S PALACE

One of my favorite memories as a kid was going to New Orleans with my dad, and one of my favorite places to go in that magical city was the Commander's Palace restaurant. It was one of my dad's favorites, too, and we always got Bananas Foster for dessert. Seeing those bananas go up in flames made quite an impression on me. Heck, that might be why I'm still fond of lighting things on fire, especially at parties.

Bananas Foster is still my favorite dessert, so, of course, there's a recipe for that in this chapter full of sweet things. But that's not the only thing I got out of those special trips to New Orleans with my father. Usually a nighttime walk along Bourbon Street would end up at the famous French Quarter venue at 726 St. Peter Street, Preservation Hall, where we would listen to all those great Dixieland jazz bands. Those musical memories were a huge inspiration, and before I moved to Nashville, I spent a year playing in the bars and on the streets of New Orleans.

On Bourbon Street I played from nine o'clock at night until six o'clock in the morning. When I got off work, I would go to an old warehouse down on the river. It was just down the street from Café Du Monde, the famous café au lait and beignet place. Every morning, night-shift workers, musicians, and bartenders would make that warehouse their last stop before calling it a night (or day). Hundreds of people would be hanging out there, drinking, rapping, talking, laughing, smoking, and basically blowing off steam until around eleven o'clock when we'd all call it quits and go home to sleep until the late shift started all over again. I won't go in to all the gory details about everything I saw during my stint in the The Big Easy, but New Orleans is an old-school voodoo kind of place, where all kinds of dark, seductive, crazy things have been going on since the beginning of time. You can feel that energy when you're there, and it doesn't compare to anything else I've ever experienced.

I guess I'll always have a soft spot in my heart for the city and its culture, especially its music and food. Somehow it seems fitting to share this story going into this chapter, which I'm calling Sweets and Indulgences. New Orleans is indulgent at its core with rich food and a rich history. And there's certainly nothing wrong with indulging every once in awhile.

# DESSERT WINE-PAIRING TIPS

*KIX STORY*: In this chapter we have everything from Bananas Foster to Beignets with Homemade Peach Ice Cream to Chocolate Praline Pecan Pie. Good coffee and tea are always great with a piece of pie or cake, but sometimes it is fun to bring out the dessert wine. And remember, dessert wines don't have to be sweet.

My winery partner and winemaker Kip Summers and I hosted a wine pairing at Cork and Cow, a really nice restaurant in Franklin, Tennessee, where we paired Syrah and chocolate cake. Syrah has a bold, rich quality that lives very easily in the world of chocolate. Amaze your friends by pulling out that combo at the end of a nice meal. Try Syrah with Heavenly Hash Cake or Mrs. Chase's Brownies (see recipes in this chapter).

Here are a few other wine/sweet pairings to consider as well:

*SAUVIGNON BLANC*: The green-skinned sauvignon blanc grape originates from the Bordeaux region of France. The crisp, elegant, and fresh flavor would complement any dessert with lemon (see the Lemon Squares recipe in this chapter).

*PROSECCO OR CHAMPAGNE*: The Italian white wine prosecco and the sparkling wine from France we know as champagne are both nice palate cleansers. Their effervescence also pairs well with a dessert like the Amazing Coconut Cake (see recipe in this chapter).

*MERLOT*: Merlot is one of the most popular red wine varietals on the market. If you find a good medium-bodied merlot with fresh, red fruit flavors, think recipes with raspberries or strawberries, like Summer Strawberry Shortcakes (see recipe in this chapter).

*Fired-Up Bananas
Foster (page 177)*

# FIRED-UP BANANAS FOSTER

*KIX STORY*: I figured we should start off the sweets chapter with my favorite dessert, Bananas Foster. First a little history lesson: Bananas Foster was invented by Paul Blange at Brennan's Restaurant in New Orleans in 1951. At that time, New Orleans was a major hub for the import of South American bananas. The dish was named for Richard Foster, chairman of the New Orleans Crime Commission and a friend of restaurant owner Owen Brennan. While Bananas Foster was invented at Brennan's, it has also been served for years at the famous Commander's Palace restaurant in New Orleans, which was taken over by the Brennan family in the 1970s. Famous chefs like Emeril Lagasse and Paul Prudhomme have called Commander's Palace home and helped make it the world-class restaurant it is to this day.

If you read the introduction to this chapter you know that I have fond memories of going to Commander's Palace with my dad as a young'un and having Bananas Foster for dessert. The ingredients are simple, but the show is spectacular! And yes, you can do this at home.

**2 bananas, peeled**

**1 tablespoon fresh lemon juice**

**2 tablespoons unsalted butter**

**¼ cup packed brown sugar**

**½ teaspoon vanilla extract**

**⅛ teaspoon ground cinnamon**

**1 tablespoon banana liqueur (optional)**

**¼ cup dark rum (to get a flame, you have to use something with a higher alcohol content, such as 151)**

**4 scoops vanilla ice cream**

Slice the bananas in half lengthwise, and then cut the lengths in half again if you like. Brush the banana pieces with lemon juice. Melt the butter with the sugar in a flat skillet over medium heat. Stir in the vanilla. Add the bananas, and sauté until just tender. Sprinkle with the cinnamon.

Remove the pan from the heat, and add liqueur, if using, and rum. Carefully ignite the liquid with a long match. Baste the bananas with the warm liquid until the flame burns out. Please don't burn the house down! Heck, you might want to do this outside. It's easy—just use a cast-iron skillet over the campfire.

Divide the ice cream among four bowls, and top with bananas and sauce.

❯ **Makes 4 servings.**

# BANANA PUDDIN'

*KIX STORY*: As commonplace as bananas are these days, it's hard to believe they used to be considered exotic and rare. It was only after the Civil War that bananas starting making their way into the southern United States via the Port of New Orleans. *Good Housekeeping* printed a banana pudding recipe in 1888, and the rest, as they say, is history!

*This dessert is a menu staple at "meat and three" cafes throughout the South, but even upscale restaurants all around the country aren't embarrassed to showcase this homey pudding.*

*You could cheat a little and use a boxed vanilla pudding as the base, but if you take a few minutes and do it from scratch, you're guaranteed to get compliments from the partakers.*

**1/2 cup white sugar or brown sugar (see Kix Tip)**

**1/3 cup all-purpose flour**

**1/4 teaspoon salt**

**2 cups milk, scalded (milk warmed in a saucepan until steam begins to rise)**

**3 egg yolks, beaten**

**1 teaspoon vanilla extract or 1 tablespoon bourbon (see Kix Tip)**

**1 cup heavy cream, whipped to stiff peaks (go ahead and whip the cream before starting the pudding)**

**1 (12-ounce) box vanilla wafers**

**5 ripe bananas, peeled and thinly sliced**

In a large, heavy saucepan, combine the sugar, flour, and salt. Mix well, and then gradually stir in the warmed milk. Cook over medium heat, stirring constantly, until slightly thickened.

Remove 1/4 cup of the milk mixture, and stir it very gradually into the egg yolks. Then stir the milk and egg mixture back into the pot. Cook, stirring constantly, until the mixture is fully thickened and coats a spoon.

Remove from the heat, and stir in the vanilla. Let cool completely before folding in half of the whipped cream.

*KIX TIP*: You can take this pudding up a notch by using bourbon instead of vanilla extract and brown sugar instead of white sugar. The pudding will have a deeper, richer flavor.

In a large glass or trifle bowl or individual dessert dishes, alternately layer the vanilla wafers and banana slices, pouring the pudding over each layer and ending with vanilla wafers. Spread the remaining whipped cream over the top, and chill briefly. You can crumble a few wafers and sprinkle them over the whipped cream if you want.

This is best eaten the day it's prepared and should be chilled if you're not eating it right away.

For easy transport to a picnic or tailgate party, make individual puddings in Mason jars with lids.

❯ **Makes 6 to 8 servings.**

# BEIGNETS

*Beignets are deep-fried pieces of dough, which are often sprinkled with powdered sugar and served for breakfast or as a dessert. Of course, you can add crab or cheese or herbs to your batter and make a savory beignet if you want to as well. Speaking of the batter, it can be a quick batter made with sugar, flour, milk, and perhaps baking powder. Or you can make a batter using yeast and end up with beignets resembling a regular doughnut or fried fritter. You can thank the French colonists for bringing the beignet to New Orleans, and you can visit the famous Café Du Monde in the French Quarter for a traditional breakfast of beignets and café au lait.*

**Vegetable oil, for deep-frying**
**2 eggs**
**1 1/2 cups all-purpose flour**
**3/4 cup whole milk**
**1 tablespoon sugar**

**1 teaspoon baking powder**
**1/4 teaspoon salt**
**Pinch of cinnamon or nutmeg (optional)**
**1/2 cup powdered sugar**

Pour enough oil to come halfway up the sides of a large, heavy, deep pot. Heat the oil over high heat to 360 degrees.

Whisk the eggs in a large bowl. Add the flour, milk, sugar, baking powder, and salt. Whisk well to make a smooth batter.

In batches, without crowding, drop heaping tablespoons of the batter into the hot oil. Fry, turning the beignets occasionally, until evenly browned. This could take several minutes. The best way to know if they're done is to take one out, cut it in half, and see if it's done in the middle. Use a slotted metal spoon to transfer the beignets to paper towels to drain.

*KIX TIP:* For a little something different, mix equal parts powdered sugar and cinnamon together, and sprinkle onto the freshly fried beignets. Or mix several small bowls of powdered sugar and other spices, such as cardamom, nutmeg, or even cayenne pepper, and let your guests sprinkle on the sugar of their choice.

Sift the powdered sugar onto the beignets, and serve immediately for breakfast or brunch. Or serve them as a dessert with Homemade Peach Ice Cream and Bourbon Caramel Sauce (see recipes).

❯ **Makes about 20 beignets or 4 to 5 servings.**

**KIX STORY:** I was in the recording studio one day when I got a call from Signature Airport, a small private airport in Nashville. They informed me that a Learjet had just landed and left a package for me. I asked, "What is it?" and they said, "It looks like a box of peaches!" I headed straight over there with a good idea of who might have sent them.

Ruston, Louisiana, calls itself the Peach Capital, and, of course, they have an annual Peach Festival. Ruston is also the home of my alma mater, Louisiana Tech, and it's very close to Marion, Louisiana, where my grandparents lived. I still have a lot of good friends in those parts, and believe me, they take a lot of pride in their peaches.

Fresh produce is what country living is all about. My grandparents had a big garden, of course, and if my grandfather and I weren't out fishing after his work, we'd be out in the garden picking whatever was ripe: tomatoes, okra, greens, beans, squash, and figs. And then came the magic season of the peach. This meant a road trip to Ruston because Ruston peaches are the best.

If you knew where to go, you could get those sweet Ruston peaches in a box with individual compartments so each peach was perfectly situated in its own cushiony holder. That meant peaches without brown spots or blemishes, only the finest ones. That's what peach season was all about. It's why you made the trip. As long as they were in season, those juicy peaches were on your breakfast cereal, they were baked and stewed, they showed up at almost every meal in some form or fashion, but the big payoff for any kid in that part of the country was homemade peach ice cream. Oh yeah!

These days, you can get an ice cream maker that will churn that cream for you, but back then I would fight with my cousins about who would get to turn the crank first. The ice and the rock salt all seemed so complicated and special. Like most things that are work-intensive that look like fun to kids, it wasn't long before I was ready to pass off the chore to the cousins. By the way, this is a great reason to have lots of children; ice cream making is hard work. At the end, when the paddle in the middle of the freezer was pulled out, looking like shutters dripping with cream, it was given to whoever had done the most work. That lucky kid got the first lick, and I'm here to tell ya, it was worth every turn of that crank.

Back to that Nashville Learjet peach delivery: There I stood in the airport, slurping away with peach juice running down my chin and fond childhood memories running through my mind, while I was making the phone call, "Hey James, did you just send me this box of peaches?" "Yeah, buddy, aren't they good? Best we've had in years, and I knew you'd want some!" I sure did!

# HOMEMADE PEACH ICE CREAM

1 (14-ounce) can sweetened condensed milk

1 (5-ounce) can evaporated milk

1 1/4 cups whole milk

4 medium fresh, ripe peaches, peeled and sliced, or 2 cups frozen peaches

2 tablespoons sugar

1/4 cup fresh lemon juice

1/4 teaspoon salt

3/4 cup peach nectar

Whisk all three milks together in a large bowl until blended. Cover and chill for 30 minutes.

Combine the peaches with the sugar, lemon juice, and salt in a blender or food processor, and process until smooth. Stir into the milk mixture along with the peach nectar.

Pour the mixture into the freezer canister of a 1-quart electric ice cream maker, and freeze according to manufacturer's instructions. Or dig out the old hand-crank maker, and put the kids to work.

Remove the canister, and place in freezer for 15 minutes. Transfer the ice cream to an airtight container, and freeze until firm, for 1 to 1 1/2 hours.

Remove the ice cream from freezer, and let it soften slightly before serving.

Peach ice cream is perfect with freshly fried Beignets and Bourbon Caramel Sauce.

❯ **Makes 8 servings.**

# BOURBON CARAMEL SAUCE

1 cup packed brown sugar

6 tablespoons butter, cut into small cubes

1/2 cup heavy cream

1 teaspoon vanilla extract

1 tablespoon bourbon

1 teaspoon regular salt or 1/2 teaspoon coarse salt

Place the brown sugar and butter in a saucepan over medium-low heat. Cook, whisking gently, until it starts to thicken, for about 7 minutes.

Slowly pour in the cream, vanilla, and bourbon, continuing to whisk. Increase the heat to medium-high, continuing to whisk, and bring the mixture to a boil. Boil for 1 minute. Remove from the heat, and whisk in salt. Let cool slightly. Pour into a glass container, and store in fridge for up to two weeks. You can rewarm this sauce in the microwave.

❯ **Makes about 1 cup.**

# SUMMER STRAWBERRY SHORTCAKES

*Even though this recipe is called "Summer" Strawberry Shortcakes, you can make it any time of the year that you can get ripe strawberries. Fresh, ripe, juicy strawberries are the key. Serving these individual "cakes" hot out of the oven with the strawberries and cream on top is the way to go, and they're the perfect dessert for an early summer feast, picnic, or a Fourth of July barbecue.*

**4 cups fresh, ripe strawberries, rinsed, hulled, and sliced in half**

**3 tablespoons sugar, plus more for sugaring the berries**

**2 cups all-purpose flour**

**1 tablespoon baking powder**

**1/4 teaspoon salt**

**1/2 cup unsalted butter, softened, plus more for spreading on the cakes**

**1 egg, beaten**

**2/3 cup heavy cream, half-and-half, or whole milk**

**1 cup heavy whipping cream, whipped to stiff peaks**

Preheat the oven to 450 degrees.

Place the berries in a bowl and sprinkle with sugar. The amount of sugar is truly to taste; anywhere from a tablespoon to a cup. If the berries are ripe and sweet, start with 1/4 to 1/2 cup sugar. Stir and let sit for at least 30 minutes. The sugar will bring out the juiciness of the berries.

In a large mixing bowl combine the flour, baking powder, and salt. Cut in the butter with a pastry cutter or two knives until the mixture is crumbly.

In a small bowl whisk together the egg and cream until well blended. Add to the flour mixture, and stir until completely moist.

Turn the dough onto a lightly floured surface, and knead briefly. Pat the dough to 1/4-inch thickness. Using a floured 3-inch biscuit cutter or a juice glass, cut out 6 biscuits. Place the biscuits on an ungreased baking sheet. Bake on the upper rack for about 10 minutes, until lightly brown on top.

While the biscuits are still hot, split them open, and butter each side. Spoon the berries and whipped cream onto the biscuits. These are best served warm.

*KIX TIP:* If you need to transport these shortcakes to the picnic in the park or the parking-lot party, just wrap the biscuits in foil as soon as they come out of the oven. Take your berries and whipped cream along in plastic tubs, and assemble the cakes on-site.

❷ **Makes 6 servings.**

**KIX STORY**: This section is like a two-for-one deal. We put these two recipes together because it's like a South-North version of the same recipe. They're similar in that they're both a cakey-like brownie chocolate cake, and they're both topped with marshmallow. Mrs. Chase's Brownies is a recipe from my wife, Barbara. Mrs. Chase was one of her mother's best friends, who had two daughters, one exactly Barb's older sister's age and one Barb's age. Mrs. Chase's eldest child, her son, was the first soldier from Massachusetts to die in the Vietnam War. Even though she was young when it happened, Barb tells me she remembers his funeral like it was yesterday. She also tells me that Mrs. Chase's brownies were famous and always a big hit at the church socials and fundraisers.

The Heavenly Hash Cake has a Southern history, handed down in my cowriter Donna's family for a couple of generations.

*Mrs. Chase's Brownies
(page 187)*

# MRS. CHASE'S BROWNIES

## Brownies

2 eggs

1 cup sugar

1/3 cup vegetable shortening

2 (1-ounce) squares baking chocolate

3/4 cup all-purpose flour

1/2 teaspoon baking powder

1/2 teaspoon salt

1/2 cup chopped pecans or walnuts (optional)

1/2 teaspoon vanilla extract

1 (14-ounce) jar marshmallow crème

## Frosting

1 cup powdered sugar

1 heaping teaspoon unsweetened cocoa

1 to 1 1/2 teaspoons milk

1/2 teaspoon vanilla extract

To prepare the brownies, preheat the oven to 350 degrees. Butter and flour an 8- or 9-inch square baking pan.

Beat the eggs in a mixing bowl. Gradually add the sugar, and keep beating until well combined. Melt the shortening and chocolate in a double boiler (see Kix Tip).

Sift together the flour, baking powder, and salt. Add the chocolate mixture to the egg mixture. Sift the flour mixture into chocolate mixture. Stir in the nuts and vanilla.

Bake for 25 minutes, or until a wooden pick inserted in the center comes out clean. While the brownies are warm, spread the marshmallow creme on top.

To prepare the frosting, combine the powdered sugar, cocoa, milk, and vanilla in a medium saucepan, and cook over low heat, stirring constantly, until bubbles form around edge of pan. Pour over the brownies, and spread with a knife while the frosting is still hot.

❯ **Makes 6 to 8 servings.**

# HEAVENLY HASH CAKE

## Cake

**1 cup (2 sticks) unsalted butter**

**2 cups sugar**

**4 eggs**

**1 teaspoon vanilla extract**

**1 1/2 cups all-purpose flour**

**4 tablespoons unsweetened cocoa**

**1 (16-ounce) package miniature marshmallows**

## Frosting

**1/2 cup (1 stick) butter**

**4 tablespoons unsweetened cocoa**

**6 to 8 tablespoons evaporated milk or 1/2 cup whole milk**

**1 teaspoon vanilla extract**

**3 to 3 1/2 cups powdered sugar**

To prepare the cake, preheat the oven to 350 degrees. Butter and flour a 9 x 13-inch baking pan.

Place the butter and sugar in a mixing bowl, and beat with an electric mixer on medium speed until light and fluffy, for 2 to 3 minutes. Add the eggs, one at a time, mixing well after each addition. Add the vanilla, and then add the flour and cocoa a little at a time, continuing to beat at medium-high speed until smooth. Pour the batter into the prepared pan.

Bake for 25 to 30 minutes, until a wooden pick inserted in the center comes out clean. Do not overbake. Remove the cake from the oven, and spread the marshmallows over the top of the cake immediately.

To prepare the frosting, combine the butter and cocoa in a saucepan, and cook over medium heat until the butter melts. Stir in the milk and vanilla. Remove from the heat. Slowly mix in the powdered sugar, starting with just 2 cups and beating until smooth and creamy. Add more powdered sugar until you get the consistency you want. You can also add more milk if the mixture is too thick. Pour and spread the frosting over the melted marshmallows. Garnish with chopped pecans or walnuts if desired.

**Makes 8 to 10 servings.**

KIX TIP: You can make a double boiler by placing a metal bowl on top of a saucepan with a couple of inches of simmering water in it. Just make sure the bottom of the bowl isn't touching the water in the pan. The steam rising from the simmering water will create the heat you need to melt the shortening and the chocolate without burning it.

# GARDEN CAKE

*KIX STORY*: This is another recipe from my wife, Barb. It's a favorite from her childhood, and she recommends getting the kids involved with this one. They'll love "digging" the little holes that you pour the liquid into, and it'll be easy for them to stir up the cake—kind of like an Easy Bake Oven confection, only you end up with a cake you really want to eat!

*This simple cake is also known as an eggless Devil's Food Cake. There are varying opinions and ideas about what makes a chocolate cake a Devil's Food Cake instead of just a plain ol' chocolate cake, but this one is fun because you mix it up right in the pan you're baking it in. It's a small cake, which you can dress up with a Vanilla Buttercream Frosting or keep it real simple with a sprinkle of powdered sugar on top. Serve with a glass of lemonade or ice tea with some fresh strawberries on the side, and you have a perfect snack to share with a friend or a neighbor on a sunny summer afternoon on the patio or front porch.*

1 ½ cups all-purpose flour

1 cup sugar

3 tablespoons unsweetened cocoa

1 teaspoon baking soda

½ teaspoon salt

⅓ cup melted vegetable shortening or oil

1 tablespoon distilled white vinegar

1 cup cold water

Powdered sugar or Vanilla Buttercream Frosting (see recipe), for topping (optional)

Preheat the oven to 350 degrees.

Measure the flour, sugar, cocoa, baking soda, and salt into a sifter. Sift at least twice, and the final time into a 9 x 9 baking pan. Be sure cocoa is well mixed into the other dry ingredients. Make three depressions in the dry ingredients.

Mix the shortening with the vinegar and cold water. Pour the liquid into the three depressions. Mix the liquid into the dry ingredients until well combined.

Bake for 20 to 25 minutes. Start checking for doneness after about 15 minutes by inserting a wooden pick into center of cake. When it comes out clean, the cake is done. Don't overbake.

*KIX TIP*: "Baker" Barbara says if you don't have a sifter, you can use a whisk to fluff up the dry ingredients. If you've ever wanted an excuse to get yourself a sifter, you have one now because this little cake will turn out even better if you actually sift the dry ingredients.

Remove the cake from the oven, and let it cool in the pan on a wire rack. Sprinkle powdered sugar on top, or frost the top with Vanilla Buttercream Frosting. Serve directly from pan.

❷ **Makes 6 servings.**

# VANILLA BUTTERCREAM FROSTING

*This is an easy buttercream frosting, which is referred to as "American buttercream." There are also meringue-based and custard-based buttercream frostings, which require a little more time and technique. This one is perfect for the Garden Cake; it was the frosting Barb's mom used with this cake.*

**½ cup unsalted butter, softened**
**1½ to 2 cups powdered sugar**
**1 teaspoon vanilla extract**

**2 tablespoons milk, heavy cream, or half-and-half**

Place the butter in a mixing bowl. Beat with an electric mixer at medium-high speed until smooth and lighter in color, for 3 to 5 minutes.

Add the sugar, ½ cup at a time. Beat well after each addition.

Mix in the vanilla. Add the milk, and beat on low speed. For a firmer frosting, add more sugar, ¼ cup at a time. For a softer frosting, add more milk or cream, a tablespoon at a time.

This recipe can be doubled easily, but this will make enough for the small Garden Cake.

❷ **Makes about 2 cups.**

# AMAZING COCONUT CAKE

***KIX STORY***: This recipe comes from my food partner-in-crime Donna Britt. She got it from a generous friend of hers in Nashville years ago, and that friend got it from someone else, so it's a handed down recipe that's time tested and coconut-lover approved. Even if you don't like cake, you'll like this one. I'd also go as far to say that even if you don't like coconut, you'll like this cake.

*This is the quintessential coconut cake. Multi-layered and stunning in all its coconut-whiteness, it's a perfect celebration cake for birthdays, holidays, even weddings. It's beautiful, it's moist, it's all about the coconut, and it's addictive.*

## Cake

2 3/4 cups all-purpose flour

1 teaspoon baking powder

1/2 teaspoon baking soda

1/2 teaspoon salt

1 3/4 cups sugar

1 cup (2 sticks) unsalted butter, room temperature

1 cup canned sweetened cream of coconut (such as Coco Lopez)

4 eggs, separated

1 teaspoon vanilla extract

1 cup buttermilk

Pinch of salt

## Simple Syrup

1/2 cup sugar

1/2 cup water

1/2 teaspoon of coconut extract

## Cream Cheese Frosting

2 (8-ounce) packages cream cheese, room temperature

6 cups powdered sugar

1/2 cup canned sweetened cream of coconut (or just what's left in the can you used in the cake)

1 teaspoon vanilla extract

1 teaspoon coconut extract

4 cups sweetened shredded coconut

Preheat the oven to 350 degrees. Butter and flour two 9-inch round cake pans. Or if you want four thin layers of cake, use four 9-inch cake pans.

To prepare the cake, whisk the flour, baking powder, baking soda, and salt in a mixing bowl to blend. Place the sugar, butter, and cream of coconut in large mixing bowl, and using an electric mixer, beat at medium speed until fluffy. Beat in the egg yolks and vanilla extract. On low speed, beat in flour mixture and then buttermilk, each just until blended.

Place the egg whites in a large mixing bowl. Using clean, dry beaters, beat the egg whites with a pinch of salt until stiff but not dry. Fold the beaten egg whites into the batter.

Divide the cake batter between the prepared pans. Bake the cakes for 35 to 45 minutes, until a wooden pick inserted into center comes out clean.

While the cake layers are baking, prepare the syrup. Heat the sugar and water in a saucepan over medium heat until the sugar completely dissolves. Remove from the heat, and add coconut extract.

*KIX TIP*: This cake can be prepared up to one day ahead. Cover with plastic wrap and refrigerate. Let stand at room temperature a couple of hours before serving.

When the cakes are done, poke them with a fork and brush them while still warm with the syrup. Let the cake cool in the pans. Once cooled, invert them onto waxed paper.

To prepare the frosting, place the cream cheese in a medium bowl, and beat with an electric mixer at medium speed until fluffy. Add the sugar and cream of coconut a little at a time, beating until smooth. Add the vanilla and coconut extracts, and beat until well blended.

After the cakes are completely cool, place one cake layer on cake plate. Spread 1 cup frosting over the top. Sprinkle 1 cup coconut over the frosting. Top with the second cake layer. Spread the remaining frosting over the top and sides of the cake. Sprinkle the remaining coconut over the cake, gently pressing into the sides to adhere.

❯ **Makes 10 to 12 servings.**

# BOURBON-SOAKED CELEBRATION CAKE

*KIX STORY:* Whether it's soaked in whiskey, Kentucky bourbon, or dark rum, this is a very special cake that's perfect for the holidays. We almost always have a cake like this at Christmastime at the Brooks' house. This is a dense, moist cake with a warm, rich spice flavor, and yes, you can taste the bourbon, and it's delicious. The rare cardamom spice mixes well with the ginger, cinnamon, nutmeg, and cloves but has a distinctive flavor that stands out in a special way; that flavor is the perfect match for the pear.

## Cake

3 cups all-purpose flour

2 teaspoons baking powder

1/2 teaspoon baking soda

1/2 teaspoon salt

1 tablespoon ground cardamom

1/2 teaspoon ground ginger

1/4 teaspoon ground cinnamon

1/4 teaspoon ground nutmeg

Tiny pinch of ground cloves

1 1/2 cups packed dark brown sugar

1/2 cup white sugar

3 eggs

1 teaspoon vanilla

1/2 cup unsalted butter, melted

1/2 cup Kentucky bourbon, whiskey, or dark rum

1/4 cup buttermilk, room temperature

2 pears, peeled and diced (you can substitute apples for the pears with excellent results)

## Bourbon Glaze

1/2 cup butter

1/4 cup Kentucky bourbon or your favorite whiskey

1 cup sugar

Preheat the oven to 350 degrees. Butter and flour a Bundt pan or round angel food cake pan. Smear lots of butter on the pan before flouring it, especially if you're using a Bundt pan. Even the nonstick Bundt pans are likely to stick a bit if you don't butter 'em up real good!

To prepare the cake, in a medium bowl, stir together the flour, baking powder, baking soda, salt, cardamom, ginger, cinnamon, nutmeg, and cloves. In a large bowl, mix together the sugars, eggs, vanilla, and butter.

Alternately add the flour mixture, bourbon, and buttermilk to the sugar mixture, beginning and ending with the flour. Add the flour in three parts and the whiskey and buttermilk in two. Mix until just combined. Stir in the pears. Pour the batter into the prepared pan, and smooth the top. Bake for at least 1 hour and 20 minutes and up to 1 hour and 45 minutes on the center rack of the oven. Halfway through the baking time, rotate the pan. The cake is done when a knife inserted into the center of the cake comes out with only a few crumbs. The top should be golden brown and cracking.

While the cake is baking, prepare the glaze. Melt the butter in a small saucepan over medium heat. Whisk in the bourbon and sugar. Reduce the heat to low, and simmer for 4 to 5 minutes.

Poke holes in the warm cake, and spread three-quarters of the glaze over the cake while still in the pan. Allow the cake to cool in pan for 30 minutes. Then loosen the sides of the cake with a thin knife, and invert the cake onto a plate. Take your time loosening the cake from the sides of the Bundt pan. It may not release on your first try at turning it over. Keep working the knife around the sides and gently tapping the bottom of the inverted pan, and it should release as long as you buttered it up like crazy beforehand! Spread the remaining glaze over the top of cake, and let it cool completely.

Wrapped well in plastic wrap or foil, this cake will stay good for several days.

❯ **Makes 10 to 12 servings.**

# KING CAKE

*KIX STORY*: Did somebody say Mardi Gras? Party? Hey, life is a celebration, and you don't have to wait till Fat Tuesday to put on your dancing shoes and party hat. Go ahead, bake a King Cake now, and share it with your friends and neighbors. This is a great brunch or breakfast cake since it resembles a cinnamon roll.

*The "season" for King Cake typically extends from the festival of Epiphany (January 6) until Fat Tuesday or Mardi Gras, the day before Ash Wednesday, which is the start of Lent for many Christian denominations.*

*King Cake is really more like a sweet dough or bread than a cake. It often has a cinnamon filling inside and is topped with colored sugars. Hundreds of thousands are eaten in New Orleans during the Carnival season.*

*The original tradition was to stow a bean inside the cake. These days, there's usually a figurine or a small plastic baby (said to represent Baby Jesus) inside or underneath the cake. Whoever gets the piece of cake with the baby inside may get various privileges or have certain obligations to fulfill, like baking the King Cake for next year's party.*

*The sugar on top is typically colored purple, green, and gold, the traditional Mardi Gras colors.*

## Cake

2 (½-ounce) packages active dry yeast
½ cup sugar
8 tablespoons unsalted butter, melted
5 egg yolks
1 cup warm milk (110 degrees)
4 to 5 cups all-purpose flour
2 teaspoons salt
1 teaspoon ground nutmeg
1 teaspoon grated lemon zest
Vegetable oil

## Filling and Sugar Glaze

2 (8-ounce) packages cream cheese
5 cups powdered sugar, divided
Juice of 2 lemons
4 tablespoons milk
Purple, green, and gold sanding sugar
Plastic baby figurine or fava bean

Preheat the oven to 350 degrees.

To prepare the cake, combine the yeast, sugar, butter, and egg yolks in a mixing bowl. Add the milk. Attach the dough hook to an electric mixer (if you don't have a dough hook, you can use regular beaters). Mix on low speed for about 4 minutes to dissolve the yeast; it should begin to foam.

In a large bowl, combine 4 cups of the flour, salt, nutmeg, and lemon zest. Add the flour mixture to the yeast mixture. Mix on low speed until the dough starts to come together, then increase the speed to medium, and mix until the dough pulls away from the sides of the bowl and forms a ball that climbs slightly up the dough hook. If the dough is too wet, add more flour, a bit at a time. (If you do not have a mixer with a dough hook, once you mix the flour mixture with the yeast mixture, remove the dough from the bowl and knead by hand on a lightly floured surface, adding in more flour if needed to make the dough easy to handle. You'll need to knead it for about 10 minutes, until it's smooth and springy.)

Oil a large bowl. Remove the dough from the mixing bowl, and place it in the oiled bowl. Coat the top of the dough with vegetable oil, turning the dough to coat all sides. Cover the bowl with plastic wrap, and place in a warm place to rise until doubled in size. If you use regular yeast, this rising will take about 2 hours. If you use rapid rising yeast, the doubling in size may take less time.

While the dough is rising, make the filling and glaze. In a small bowl combine the cream cheese and 1 cup of the powdered sugar. Mix well.

In a medium bowl, combine the remaining 4 cups of powdered sugar, lemon juice, and milk to make the sugar glaze. Mix well and set aside.

*Kix Tip:* If the yeast doesn't foam, it isn't active, and you'll need to start over with fresh yeast.

Turn the risen dough onto a floured surface, and roll out 30 inches long and 6 inches across. Measure it for best results; you want a long, narrow piece of dough. Spread the cream cheese filling down the middle of the dough. Bring the two long sides together, and pinch to seal completely. Shape the dough into a long cylinder, and place on a greased baking sheet seam side down. Shape the dough into a ring. Place a well-buttered 2-pound empty coffee can or other can in the center of the ring to maintain the shape of the ring during baking.

Press the plastic baby figurine or bean into the ring of dough from the bottom so that is it completely hidden. Cover the ring with a towel, and place in a warm place to rise until dough doubles in size, for about 45 minutes.

With a sharp knife, make several slits around the top of the ring. Bake for 25 to 35 minutes, until golden brown. After baking remove the can immediately and let the cake cool on the baking pan.

Drizzle the cake with the sugar glaze and sprinkle with sanding sugars, alternating the colors.

❷ **Makes 10–12 servings.**

# OATMEAL COOKIES

*KIX STORY*: Oatmeal cookies are my favorite. I think that's because oatmeal makes me think I'm eating something healthy. Oatmeal, raisins, nuts, honey—hey, that's all healthy stuff. It's actually the honey that gives these cookies a nice texture, somewhere between too crispy and too soft.

You can make the cookies any size you want—just adjust the baking time for larger or smaller. Any size works for spreading ice cream in the middle to make ice cream sandwiches (see recipe). Make up the sandwiches and store them in plastic ziptop bags in the freezer. When the kids or grandkids show up and you need a quick dessert, there you go!

**1 cup unsalted butter, softened**
**1 3/4 cups packed brown sugar**
**2 eggs**
**1/3 cup honey**
**1 1/2 cups all-purpose flour**
**4 cups old-fashioned rolled oats**

**1 1/2 teaspoons ground cinnamon**
**1/2 teaspoon salt**
**1 1/2 cups coarsely chopped walnuts or pecans (optional)**
**1 1/2 cups raisins**

Preheat the oven to 400 degrees with rack in center of oven.

Combine the butter and sugar in a large mixing bowl. Using an electric mixer, beat on medium-high speed until light and fluffy, about 5 minutes. Beat in the eggs one at a time with mixer on low speed. Mix in the honey.

Whisk the flour, oats, cinnamon, and salt together in a separate bowl. Gradually add the flour mixture to the butter mixture, stirring with a wooden spoon or with the mixer on low speed. Mix until no flour is visible. Stir in the nuts and raisins.

Drop spoonfuls of dough onto an ungreased baking sheet about 2 inches apart. There's no need to flatten the cookie dough. Bake for 10 to 12 minutes for smaller cookies and up to 15 to 18 minutes for large cookies. Check after about 8 minutes because cooking times can vary a lot. You don't want to overcook, or they'll be hard once they've cooled.

Place the pan on a wire rack to cool slightly, then transfer the cookies to the rack to cool completely.

*KIX TIP*: You can put parchment paper on your baking sheets, so that when you take cookies out of oven, all you have to do is slide the paper with the baked cookies off the baking sheet and onto a flat surface to cool.

❯ **Makes about 4 dozen small cookies.**

# ICE CREAM SANDWICHES

**1 recipe Oatmeal Cookies**
**Vanilla ice cream, slightly softened**

**Sprinkles and chocolate chips
(optional)**

After the cookies have cooled completely, place a spoonful of ice cream onto the bottom of one of the cookies. Place another cookie on top to make a sandwich. You can use any flavor ice cream you want. You can also roll the sandwiches in sprinkles or chocolate chips or whatever sounds good. Place sandwiches on a plate or small baking sheet, and wrap with plastic wrap. Return to freezer if you're not serving immediately.

# LEMON SQUARES

**KIX STORY:** My wife, Barbara, is usually the one who bakes at our house. Her recipe for Lemon Squares is one she has written down on a small index card that's been in the recipe collection for years. I'm not sure where it came from, but you can tell by the splatters and tatters on that little recipe card that it's a favorite of ours.

*Whether you call them "squares" or "bars," these are easy to whip up. If you don't have fresh lemons lying around for squeezing, you could cheat and use the bottled lemon juice. Nobody has to know!*

## Crust

**2 cups all-purpose flour**

**1 cup powdered sugar**

**Pinch of salt**

**1 cup (2 sticks) unsalted butter, room temperature**

## Filling

**4 eggs**

**2 cups white sugar**

**6 tablespoons all-purpose flour**

**6 tablespoons freshly squeezed lemon juice**

**Powdered sugar**

Preheat the oven to 350 degrees. Butter a 9 x 13-inch baking pan.

To prepare the crust, combine the flour, powdered sugar, and salt in a large bowl. Cut in the butter with a pastry blender or two knives to make a crumbly mixture. Press the mixture into the prepared pan. Bake for 20 minutes, or until lightly browned.

To prepare the filling, mix the eggs, white sugar, flour, and lemon juice. Pour over the baked crust, and bake for 25 minutes. Sprinkle with powdered sugar when done. Cut into squares when cooled.

❯ **Makes 12 servings.**

# CHOCOLATE PRALINE PECAN PIE

**KIX STORY:** My dad's family was from Fort Necessity, a community in Franklin Parish, Louisiana, with a population of less than a hundred. My brother and I still own the farm where our people came from, which is a piece of land that has been in my family since 1807. There are 200-year-old pecan trees still standing and still producing on that property. This recipe is a salute to those beautiful, ancient trees and to the iconic Southern confection known as the praline, pronounced *prah-leen* (just so you know).

*Pecans are the only nut indigenous to the South. Georgia harvests more pecans than any other state (more than one million pounds per year), while Louisiana is credited with the successful grafting of pecan trees and for using the strategically placed Port of New Orleans for the global export of the pecan.*

*The praline migrated from France to the banks of the Mississippi River. Pecans were substituted for almonds, and cream was added, and a Southern tradition was born. Today, pralines can be found in just about every convenience store and supermarket around New Orleans, and there are praline specialty shops throughout the French Quarter.*

2 cups heavy cream

1/4 cup cornstarch

1/2 cup packed brown sugar

1/2 cup light corn syrup

1 cup semisweet chocolate morsels, melted

1 (9-inch) piecrust, blind baked and chilled (see Basic Pie Pastry recipe in this chapter), or 1 (9-inch) store-bought chocolate graham cracker crust, chilled

1 cup crumbled Pralines (see recipe)

1 cup Toasted Pecans (see recipe, optional)

Whipped cream, for serving (optional)

Combine the heavy cream, cornstarch, brown sugar, and syrup in a medium, heavy saucepan. Cook over medium-high heat, whisking constantly, until a slightly thick custard forms, for 10 to 12 minutes. Stir in the chocolate morsels, and mix well. Remove from the heat. Place a piece of waxed paper directly on top of the custard, and let cool completely. The waxed paper will keep a film from forming on the custard.

Remove the piecrust from refrigerator.

Fold the crumbled Pralines into the cooled custard. Pour the mixture into the crust. Arrange Toasted Pecan halves on top, if using.

Cover with plastic wrap, and chill in fridge for at least 4 hours before serving. Serve with whipped cream if desired.

❍ **Makes 6 to 8 servings.**

# TOASTED PECANS

**2 cups pecan halves**

**2 tablespoons unsalted butter, melted**

**1 tablespoon white or raw sugar**

Preheat the oven to 325 degrees.

Toss the pecans with the butter and sugar, and spread on a baking sheet. Bake for about 25 minutes, shaking the pan frequently, until lightly browned.

❍ **Makes 2 cups.**

# PRALINES

**1 cup packed brown sugar**

**1/2 cup white sugar**

**1/2 cup heavy cream**

**4 tablespoons unsalted butter**

**2 tablespoons water**

**Pinch of salt**

**1 1/2 cups chopped pecans**

**1 teaspoon vanilla extract**

Line a large baking sheet with wazed or parchment paper.

Combine the sugars, cream, butter, water, and salt in a heavy saucepan over medium heat. Cook, stirring to dissolve the sugar, for 3 to 4 minutes. Let the mixture come to a boil. Add the pecans, and continue cooking and stirring for another 5 minutes.

Remove from the heat, and stir in vanilla. Drop by spoonfuls onto the waxed paper. Let cool.

Pralines can be stored in airtight container at room temperature for two weeks.

*KIX TIP:* If you want to stock up on pecans while they're in season, shell them and freeze them in tightly sealed plastic bags for up to nine months.

# BASIC PIE PASTRY

*This is the pastry dough that you can use for the Chocolate Praline Pecan Pie in this book and for any other pie you want to make that calls for a regular piecrust.*

2 cups all-purpose flour

2 pinches of salt

1 ½ cups butter-flavored vegetable shortening

⅔ cup ice water

Mix the flour and salt in large bowl. Cut in the shortening with a pastry cutter or two knifes. Add the water a bit at a time. Work in extra flour if necessary until dough is soft and pliable. Touch the dough. Feel it. This is a hands-on thing. Divide the dough in half. Wrap each half in plastic wrap, and chill for at least 30 minutes or until ready to use.

To blind bake the crust, preheat the oven to 400 degrees.

Remove the chilled dough from fridge. Once it's warmed up enough to be pliable, press it into a pie pan, fluting the crust however you prefer. Bake for 10 to 15 minutes, until it's just beginning to turn tan. Remove from oven, and let it cool. Then wrap in plastic wrap, and store in refrigerator until ready to use.

❯ **Makes 2 piecrusts.**

# CHAPTER 8
# LIBATIONS, COCKTAILS, AND BEVERAGES

# FILLING UP THE JAR

*I* always think of the chain that Elvis Presley used to wear around his neck that had the letters TCB on it. TCB—Taking Care of Business.

There's on old story where, on a table, you have a stack of rocks along with a big pickle jar. There is gravel on your right and a pile of sand to the left. While there's room for everything in the jar, it's important to lay the big rocks in there first. You shake the gravel in around the big rocks. Once the big rocks and the gravel are in there, you pour in the sand to fill the jar completely. If you put the sand and the gravel in first, the big rocks won't fit.

The point is priorities. When you start your day, decide what the big rocks are, what's important to you, what your priorities are, and take care of that big "business" first (i.e., Elvis's necklace). Don't waste time with the sand (the lesser priorities) and not be able to get your jar full.

I've heard a version of the jar-rocks-sand story where you can pour a beer in the jar after you put the sand in, which proves no matter how full your day is, there's still room for a cold one.

This chapter has some great ideas for celebratory cocktails and party drinks as well as a nice variety of drinks with just juice and lemons and tea—something for everyone I would say. Cheers!

# COCKTAIL BASICS

*KIX STORY*: My entire family is a bunch of showoffs! My dad was an unbelievable storyteller who could hold an audience at conventions or right there in the living room at home. As a kid, I would hear him tell the same story ten or fifteen times, and each time he told it, it would get a little bit better.

We all sang as much as we talked in our family too. We knew a million songs, and every summer that I stayed at my grandparents' house in Marion, where there wasn't anything but a couple of general stores and a bookmobile that came around every other week, we entertained each other. Every evening we'd put on a show before dinnertime. As my grandparents sipped their pre-dinner cocktails, the kids (my cousins and I) would decide which songs to sing and which stories to tell, and we'd put on a show. That was just a part of our daily routine. It's in that spirit of entertainment and camaraderie that I share a few of my favorite cocktails and beverages with you.

I like to keep it simple but still make my guests feel special if I'm throwing a party or a get-together. I'm no expert bartender, but here are a couple of tips that I think might come in handy if you're the one in charge of the drinks.

## KIX TIPS:

- Rather than ounces and other exact measurements for drinks, it's easier to think proportions. One part alcohol to two parts juice is fairly standard for straightforward drinks like a Screwdriver, for example.
- Use big ice cubes. They look cool, and they melt more slowly than regular ice cubes. You can find trays for bigger-sized ice cubes in most grocery or discount stores these days.
- Garnish your drink even if it's a mocktail or an iced tea. People eat (and drink) with their eyes first.
- Just like quality ingredients make the difference with food, quality ingredients also make the difference with drinks. Fresh juices and fresh fruit and the best liquors you can afford will make your drinks delicious and memorable.
- A red Solo cup is just about perfect for almost any drink you'll be serving at your tailgating party or out on the deck on the Fourth of July, but keep a few special cocktail glasses on hand too. You don't have to get overly fancy, but sometimes it is fun to show off your creations, and a pretty glass will do that for you!
- Another great thing to know how to do is to make a Simple Syrup, which is used to sweeten numerous drinks. It's equal parts water and sugar heated together until the sugar dissolves. It keeps in the fridge for a few weeks, so you can make some up and have it on hand for those unexpected, last-minute, "hey, let's celebrate" times. You can also add things to your simple syrup to make it extra special, such as mint, cinnamon, rosemary, or peppers. Here's a recipe to get you started on that fun.

# MINT-INFUSED SIMPLE SYRUP

1 cup water

1 cup sugar

1 cup loosely packed fresh mint leaves

Bring the water to a boil in a medium saucepan. Reduce the heat to low. Add the sugar and mint, and simmer until the sugar is completely dissolved, for about 2 minutes. Remove from the heat, and let cool completely. Pour the syrup through a fine wire-mesh strainer into a lidded jar or other airtight container, discarding mint. This will keep in refrigerator for up to two weeks.

# SCOTCH ON THE ROCKS

*KIX STORY*: If you have a good Scotch whiskey in your cupboard, serving it on the rocks is a great way to let the whiskey take center stage. A couple of ice cubes can actually bring out the flavor of the whiskey, although some people don't like the melting ice to dilute their drink. One solution to that is to get some whiskey stones, which you can put in the freezer. They're usually made of soapstone or some kind of substance that doesn't melt, so they chill your drink without watering it down.

There's an old legend about how Scots used to chill their whiskey with stones cooled in the rivers and creeks. They would dig the small pebbles out of the earth right there by the rivers, chill them in the water, and then pour their whiskey over them. In Europe, bars often serve Scotch over metal "ice" cubes.

**Chilled whiskey stones (optional)**
**Ice cube(s)**

**Scotch whiskey**

Put a few whiskey stones or one large ice cube into a glass. Pour scotch slowly into the glass to cover the stones or ice.

❯ **Makes 1 drink.**

*KIX TIP*: You can add a splash of water or club soda to the Scotch if you want to. There's no right or wrong way; it's simply a matter of taste.

# MANHATTAN

*KIX STORY*: This classic cocktail is believed to have originated at the Manhattan Club in New York City in the 1870s. It may have first been made with rye whiskey, but I prefer bourbon for my Manhattan, as do most folks in the South. Proportions are two parts whiskey to one part sweet vermouth with a little aromatic boost from bitters.

Ice

2 dashes Angostura bitters

1 ounce sweet vermouth

2 ounces bourbon (or rye whiskey)

1 cherry, either a maraschino cherry or a cherry in marasca syrup (see Kix Tip)

Fill a cocktail shaker two-thirds full of ice. Add the bitters, vermouth, and bourbon. Shake, shake, shake the shaker. Pour the liquid, minus the ice, into a martini glass or short cocktail glass. Add the cherry, and crush it against the side of the glass with a spoon. Stir.

❯ Makes 1 drink.

*KIX TIP*: Cherries in marasca syrup are a special variety of sour cherries that have been candied and preserved in a booze-infused cherry syrup. Think of them as the original, handmade maraschino cherry—no artificial colors or flavors. You can find them in specialty stores and online. They're worth tracking down if you ask me.

# KB'S GO-TO MOSCOW MULE

*KIX STORY:* At the time I'm writing this, my go-to drink on a random evening at the house is a Moscow Mule. It's a simple drink made with three ingredients including ginger beer. I like having ginger beer on hand because it goes with everything. You can mix it with vodka and lime juice and have yourself a Mule, of course. You could also mix it with spiced rum to make a Dark-n-Stormy, the national drink of Bermuda. Ginger beer also goes with tequila and even bourbon. Bourbon, ginger beer, and cherries on the rocks—try that!

**Ice**

**One part vodka**

**Juice of 1/4 to 1/2 lime or lemon**

**Two to three parts ginger beer**

**Lime wedge**

**Mint sprig**

Fill a metal cup with ice (use a specially made Moscow Mule mug if you have one). Add the vodka and juice. Top with the ginger beer. Garnish with a lime wedge and mint sprig.

❯ **Makes 1 drink.**

*KIX TIP:* It's best to mix one drink at a time in order to keep the ginger beer from getting watered-down and diluted, although if you're expecting a crowd and no one wants to play bartender, you could go ahead and make up a pitcher of the lime juice and vodka mixed together. Pour that mixture over ice into individual metal cups, then top each off with the ginger beer and garnish.

# BLOOD-ORANGE MADRAS (AND MOCKTAIL)

*KIX STORY*: This drink is like a Tequila Sunrise minus the grenadine syrup. I prefer the Madras because it calls for cranberry juice, which I like because it's less sweet than grenadine. Both the blood orange and the cranberry juice are full of vitamin C, and the cranberry juice is also a good source of vitamins E and K. So I say take your vitamins!

*The blood orange may have originated in China or the Southern Mediterranean, where they have been growing since the eighteenth century. They are now the primary orange variety grown in Italy. They're famous for their crimson-colored flesh.*

**Ice**
**One part tequila**
**One part unsweetened cranberry juice**
**One part blood orange juice**

**Splash of soda water (optional)**
**Orange slices**
**Maraschino cherries**

Fill a Collins or hurricane glass all the way with ice. Pour the tequila over the ice. Then pour in the juices, one at a time. Top with a splash of soda water if you want to give it some fizz. Garnish with an orange slice and maraschino cherries.

For a mocktail, just leave out the tequila.

❯ **Makes 1 drink.**

# GRAPEFRUIT-BASIL SANGARITA

*This is a hybrid sangria-margarita, which goes over extremely well with both sangria and margarita lovers. This drink is a perfect beverage to serve with the Taco Bar spread in chapter 4. It makes a big batch that you can serve from a pitcher or punch bowl.*

3 ³/₄ cups fresh grapefruit juice (5 grapefruits)

2 cups fresh orange juice (4 oranges)

1 (.75-liter) bottle white wine (Riesling or any white wine of your choice)

1 (1-liter) bottle sparkling water (like San Pellegrino)

½ cup maple syrup

3 tablespoons sugar

¼ cup triple sec

¼ cup brandy

Handful of chopped fresh basil

6 to 8 ounces tequila

Orange and grapefruit slices and wedges

Basil leaves

Salt and sugar, for rimming glasses (optional)

Mix the fruit juices, wine, and water together in a big pitcher. Mix the syrup, sugar, triple sec, and brandy in another container, then pour into the juice mixture. Stir in the basil. Chill for at least 6 hours or overnight. Strain into another pitcher or punch bowl. Pour in the tequila.

Add slices of grapefruit and oranges to the pitcher or punch bowl.

Pour into wine glasses or any other glass over ice, and place a sprig of basil on top.

If you want to rim glasses first, pour equal amounts of salt and sugar onto a small saucer or plate. Rub the rim of each glass with a wedge of fresh orange or grapefruit, then press the damp rim onto the salt-sugar mixture. Pour the drink into rimmed glass, and garnish with an orange or grapefruit slice or wedge and basil sprig.

❍ **Makes 6 to 8 servings.**

> *KIX TIP:* A combination of freshly squeezed fruit juices and canned juice works well for this recipe. If you want to use only freshly squeezed juice, do it. Otherwise, it will taste great with canned or bottled juices or a combination of fresh and canned.

# GRAPEFRUIT-BASIL SANGARITA MOCKTAIL

3 ¾ cups fresh grapefruit juice
   (5 grapefruits)

2 cups fresh orange juice (4 oranges)

1 (1-liter) bottle White Grape Juice

1 (1-liter) bottle sparkling water (like
   San Pellegrino)

½ cup maple syrup

3 tablespoons sugar

Handful of chopped fresh basil

Orange and grapefruit slices and
   wedges

Mix the fruit juices and sparkling water together in big pitcher. Mix the syrup and sugar in another container, then pour in with the juice mixture. Stir in the basil. Let chill for at least 6 hours or overnight. Strain into another pitcher or punch bowl. Add slices of grapefruit and oranges to the pitcher or punch bowl.

❷ **Makes 6 to 8 servings.**

# BOURBON SLUSHIES

*KIX STORY*: This recipe is a favorite from my recipe tester and editor, Donna Britt. Donna grew up between two lakes in Northern Arkansas and her momma, Ms. Patsy, still lives on one of the lakes there. Throughout the summer when "the (grown) kids" come for visits, Patsy makes up batches of these Slushies.

Funny thing is she's not much of a drinker, so how she came up with a frozen cocktail that tastes this great is beyond all of us! I do need to warn you that these yummy, icy things are potent, and they go down easy on a hot, humid Southern summer day, so you might want to limit yourself to only one or two!

*This is a great make-ahead, crowd-pleasing drink, perfect for hot summer days on the lake or at the beach.*

1 (12-ounce) can frozen orange juice

1 (6-ounce) can frozen lemonade

2 cups brewed ice tea (see Southern Tea recipe)

6 cups water

1 cup sugar

2 cups bourbon, or maybe even a little more

Mix the juice concentrates, tea, water, sugar, and bourbon together in a freezer-proof container. Freeze for 2 hours, and then stir. Put back in freezer immediately, and freeze for at least a full day. Remove from freezer, and place in a cooler or ice chest if you're headed out to the lake. When you're ready to serve, scrape the icy mixture into cups or glasses.

Bourbon Slushies are perfect scooped into a plastic cup. And it's good to put a straw into each cup, which can be used for stirring the drink as it melts.

This recipe can easily be doubled if you're expecting a bigger crowd.

*KIX TIP*: Make sure you take a big spoon or some kind of scooper with you if you're taking this drink outdoors. You'll need something to use to scrape it out of the container. It's never frozen solid (thanks to the alcohol), but it won't pour either.

❯ **Makes 8 to 10 servings.**

# HOLIDAY MILK PUNCH

*KIX STORY*: Ronnie Dunn and I were invited to be part of the entertainment one year for the Krewe of Endymion's after-parade party (the Endymion Extravaganza) in the New Orleans Superdome. The Krewe of Endymion's parade is one of Mardi Gras' largest and is known for having celebrity grand marshalls. My wife, Barbara, and Ronnie's wife, Janine, also got to ride on the Krewe of Endymion's float that year, and from what I remember, they were the first women to ever get to ride on one of the krewe's floats. What Barb remembers is that the parade lasted about seven hours. And no, there were no bathroom breaks. I think she might have had several glasses of milk punch once she finally made it off that float and into the Superdome for the Brooks & Dunn show.

*Milk punch is a cocktail that dates back to the eighteenth century. Back in the day, milk got mixed with liquor, simple syrup, and dairy-curdling citrus, and then those curds were strained out, leaving behind flavorful alcohol-infused whey. Before refrigeration this process ensured the punch remained good on the shelf for months.*

*Milk punch is still a New Orleans tradition, the beverage of choice for the fellows working the Mardi Gras floats. Fat Tuesday can be a very long day for those guys, up early for the parade and up until the wee hours attending a ball.*

1/2 cup skim milk

2 tablespoons half-and-half

1 teaspoon vanilla extract

2 ounces spiced rum or bourbon

Splash of Drambuie liqueur

Cracked ice

4 teaspoons powdered sugar

Freshly grated nutmeg

Pour the milk, half-and-half, vanilla, rum, and liqueur over cracked ice in a cocktail shaker or lidded jar. Spoon in the sugar, and then shake vigorously. Pour into a large old-fashioned glass or martini glass, and sprinkle nutmeg on top.

❱ **Makes 1 drink.**

*KIX TIP*: Ground nutmeg is fine to sprinkle on top of this drink, but if you have fresh nutmeg lying around, grate some of that on top to make it fancy and even more delicious!

# GINGER MO'

I'm not a big fan of the traditional mojito with rum and sugar and mint. It's usually a little too sweet for me. But I do like ginger, and this combo of ginger and mint and lime is not too sweet. It's a refreshing drink, and including a slice of fresh ginger with the garnish is a fun and different twist that will get your guests' attention.

½ cup fresh mint leaves

½ inch piece of fresh ginger, unpeeled, cut into 2 or 3 pieces

Ice cubes

¼ cup fresh lime juice

¼ cup white rum

¼ cup Simple Syrup (see recipe in Cocktail Basics)

Club soda (optional)

Mint sprigs

Limes, cut into thin slices

Fresh ginger, peeled, cut into thin slices

Place the fresh mint, ginger pieces, and a handful of ice in a big glass or large cocktail shaker. Muddle it well, as you want to break up the ginger into little bits and release the oil from the mint. Add the lime juice, rum, simple syrup, and more ice to fill the shaker, and shake, shake, shake!

Pour into four glasses, and splash a bit of club soda on top, if using. Add more ice to each glass if you want.

Garnish each glass with a slice of lime, a thin slice of fresh ginger, and a mint sprig stacked together on a cocktail pick or a toothpick.

❯ **Makes 4 drinks.**

*KIX TIP:* There is some debate about how to muddle properly. For this mojito, you muddle the mint together with the ginger and the ice. Another way to muddle, and some might say it's the more proper way, is to muddle the leaves alone, with no ice. The choice is yours, and you could try it both ways and see how each method affects the flavor and decide which you like best.

# GINGER MO' MOCKTAIL

**2 fresh mint leaves**
**1 tablespoon fresh lime juice**
**1 teaspoon sugar**

**Ice cubes**
**Splash of ginger ale**
**Splash of club soda**

In a tall glass, gently muddle together the mint leaves and lime juice. Add the sugar, and fill the glass with ice cubes. Add the ginger ale and club soda, and stir well. Garnish with a lime wedge and mint sprig.

❷ **Makes 1 drink.**

**KIX STORY:** At this point, I don't even know how many times I've been to the Kentucky Derby, but Churchill Downs is home to some of my favorite memories. My father had racehorses when I was a kid—nothing too fancy, but I did learn to read a racing form somewhere around seven or eight years old. His owning those horses led to many fun trips to New Orleans with him to watch the "ponies run" at the Fair Grounds racetrack. Then about thirty years ago, I started making my annual journey to Louisville for the greatest of all spectacles, the Kentucky Derby!

I've done the Derby just about every way you can think of—from partying with college pals in the grandstands to rocking with the crazies in the infield. (I actually pushed my way to the fence with my wife, Barbara, and watched the great Willie Shoemaker win his last Derby.) About twenty years ago I got an invitation from Patricia Barnstable to come to a fundraiser event she does with her sister every year that includes a party the night before and great seats to the Derby the next day. A tradition was born.

Since then, I've gone to Patricia's event almost every year. The namedropping I can do from all the years at the event is over the top—from Kid Rock to Jewel to Smoky Robinson. One year we sat with Dennis Hopper and the entire Manning family, Peyton, Eli, Archie, and the rest. Last year I jammed with my buddies Dierks Bentley and Miranda Lambert at the party before the big race, and I could go on and on. But the one time that will rest soft and sacred in my memory forever was the year I took my sister, Midge, and my brother-in-law, Stewart.

Midge had been on a very tough and courageous six-year fight with breast cancer. We lost our mother to this horrible disease when we were kids, so there was no denying how serious this fight was, but she refused to let anyone feel sorry for her or let her pain or weakness get in the way of anything she wanted to do. She was getting weaker in 2013, and I knew she'd never been to the Derby even though we'd talked about going together for years. Midge had three small tumors that had grown in her brain as a result of the cancer, and they had to be removed. The only time the surgeon could do the procedure was the week of the Derby. I called her to say how sorry I was that she would have to miss our trip, but she wasn't having any of that talk! I said, "Okay, if you can do it, so can I!"

She didn't miss a thing. I had a show the night before in Louisville, and she was on the front row. We grabbed a police escort and screamed over to the Barnstable fundraiser after I came off stage, and she was in the middle of the craziest party you'd ever want to see. The next day, sporting her awesome Derby hat, she jumped in the middle of that race-day chaos like she'd never felt better! Valerie Harper (the star of the TV show *Rhoda*) was there and had also been on a well-documented battle with cancer. She and Midge became fast friends and took a minute to share their journey with each other, but that's about all the time cancer got that day.

Nobody would have ever guessed she'd had brain surgery three days before. All the money in the world couldn't buy my memory of that day and the smile on her face as we raised our mint juleps and toasted this wonderful life we got to live together. I lost my sister Midge the next year, but a Derby will never get past me without raising a glass to her and the courage God gives us to fight, if we are willing to accept it! Now, please, take this recipe with no sadness; Midge would have wanted only joy and good times attached.

# DERBY DAY MINT JULEP

**3 to 4 tablespoons superfine sugar**
**Water**
**Several sprigs of fresh mint**
**Finely crushed ice**
**2 to 3 ounces Kentucky bourbon**

Into a julep cup (yes, there's such a thing), a highball glass, or a Mason jar, press 2 tablespoons of sugar together with a very small amount of water, just enough to make a sugary paste. Add a layer of mint leaves. Press them gently with a muddler or wooden spoon.

Pile on a layer of finely crushed ice. Add a sprinkling of sugar. Slap a few mint leaves on your hand, then add them to the cup.

Top with another layer of ice and sugar, and continue the layering until the glass is completely full. Then pour in the bourbon.

*KIX TIP*: Slapping the mint sprigs on your hand is actually called "spanking." It's better to "spank" your mint than to crush it to get the mint oil to ooze out properly. Go ahead—spank your mint!

❍ **Makes 1 drink.**

# CAFÉ BRULOT

***KIX STORY*:** I have read stories that link this after-dinner spiced coffee drink to the famed early nineteenth-century Louisiana pirate Jean Lafitte; it was maybe even created by one of his lieutenants, Dominique Youx. Whether that's true or not, pirates and flames always get my attention!

Café Brulot is a spectacle and tradition in New Orleans. In the old-line Creole restaurants, making and presenting this drink to customers requires a silver brulot bowl, a tray, and a long-handled ladle. Hot coffee is ladled over a spiraled orange peel steeped in brandy, and then set on fire!

One of my favorite duck hunting retreats is Little Pecan Island way down in south Louisiana. You might not expect something like Café Brulot to show up at an out-of-the-way place like that, but there's an amazing chef down there who whips up some unbelievable food for us hunters, and he lights up the evening after dinner with his special Café Brulot.

Now, if you don't have all that exotic Café Brulot equipment and you're not sure about setting orange peels on fire in the kitchen, we've simplified this spiked coffee drink so that it's easy to make at home. You still get to light a fire though!

1 orange

12 whole cloves

1/3 cup brandy

1/3 cup Cointreau or other orange-flavored liqueur

3 (2-inch long) strips lemon zest

2 cinnamon sticks

1 tablespoon sugar

3 cups hot, very strong coffee (Café Du Monde Coffee and Chicory is excellent for this, and you can order it online)

Remove the zest from the orange in a single spiral with a sharp peeler or paring knife. Stud the orange zest with the cloves, and place it in medium, heavy saucepan. Add the brandy, Cointreau, lemon zest, cinnamon stick, and sugar, and heat over medium-low heat until warm throughout. Now, if you're feeling brave, use a long match to ignite the mixture. While flames are subsiding, slowly pour in the hot coffee. Ladle into mugs or demitasse cups.

❯ **Makes 4 servings.**

# SOUTHERN TEA

5 to 7 tea bags (some people say
   Luzianne tea is the best for real
   Southern sweet tea)
1 quart cool, filtered or bottled water

Ice
Mint sprigs
Lemon wedges

Bring the water to just below boiling. Remove from heat, and pour over the tea bags in a 4-cup glass measuring cup. Steep for exactly 9 minutes. Gently squeeze the tea bags, and remove. Pour the hot tea into a 2-quart pitcher filled with ice. Stir well. This unsweetened tea can be served in ice-filled glasses and garnished with lemons and mint leaves. If you want the sweet version, keep reading!

This basic tea recipe is a great base for other flavored teas as well as for the Bourbon Slushies (see the Bourbon Slushies recipe in this chapter).

❯ **Makes 8 servings.**

For Sweet Tea, whisk 1/2 to 1 cup sugar into the steeped tea after you've removed the tea bags. Start with 1/2 cup and taste. If you want it sweeter, add more sugar.

# PEACH TEA

5 to 7 tea bags
1 quart cool, filtered or bottled water
1 large peach, peeled, pitted, and
   chopped
1/2 cup sugar

1/3 cup fresh lemon juice
Ice
1 1/2 cups sparkling water
   (like San Pellegrino)
Lemon slices

Bring the water to just below boiling. Remove from heat, and pour over the tea bags in the 4-cup glass measuring cup. Steep for exactly 9 minutes. Gently squeeze the tea bags, and remove.

Blend the peach, sugar, and lemon juice in a blender. Add the peach puree to steeped tea. Pour into a 2-quart pitcher filled with ice. Pour the sparkling water into the pitcher. Serve with lemon slices on top.

❯ **Makes 8 servings.**

Serving ideas: Sweet Tea and the Peach Tea are excellent served in tall glasses rimmed with sugar and lemon zest. Mix $1/2$ cup sugar with the finely grated zest from $1/2$ lemon, and spread the mixture on a small saucer. Rub a lemon half around a glass to get the rim a bit wet, then dip the rim into the mixture. Fill the glass with ice, and pour in the tea.

*KIX STORY*: I know better than to get into a discussion about sweet tea. It may sound like a simple thing to make since the main ingredients are brewed black tea and sugar, but as any good Southerner will tell you, not all sweet tea is created equal. If you have your own favorite sweet tea recipe, then go ahead, turn the page, and skip my suggestions. I am not going to even try to tell you that mine is better because, heck, it might not be!

Use whatever recipe you want, but drink tea. Tea has high levels of antioxidants that help boost your body's defenses against disease. Tea may also lower blood pressure and cholesterol and protect against cancer. If you're worried about consuming sugar, leave it out or substitute honey or Stevia.

# FROTHY LEMONADE

***KIX STORY:*** I see you turning your nose up at the idea of milk in your lemonade, but this is an old-fashioned recipe that goes way back. If you don't tell anybody there's milk in it, I swear no one will know. Go on, give it a try. I'm betting you're going to like it!

*The kids are gonna love this lemonade but so will the adults. Of course, you can add a swig of vodka or rum to your cup if you're so inclined. You can always double the recipe to make a bigger batch if you've got a big, thirsty crowd on your hands.*

**2 lemons**

**1 ½ cups sugar**

**2 cups milk, skim or whole or whatever you prefer**

**3 cups chilled club soda or sparkling water**

**Additional sugar, for rimming glasses**

Juice the lemons, saving the peel and pulp. Place the peel and pulp in a blender, and process until coarsely chopped. Add the peel mixture and sugar to the lemon juice, and mix well. Let stand for 30 minutes.

Stir in the milk. Strain the mixture into a big pitcher or jar. Add the club soda. Serve in sugar-rimmed glasses over ice. Bring a big jug of this to a barbecue or tailgater, and everybody will be asking for the recipe!

❷ **Makes 8 servings.**

# FIERY APPLE CIDER

*KIX STORY*: This cider recipe was handed down from somebody in my family, although I can't remember exactly who; it's been around a long time. It's an easy drink to make for a tailgater when you need a hot drink to warm everybody up. Bring your jugs of cider to the party, and, if you dare, include a flask of Fireball Whiskey to heat things up even more!

**1 gallon apple cider**

**48 whole cloves**

**4 teaspoons ground allspice**

**4 cinnamon sticks**

**1 cup orange juice**

**1 tablespoon lemon juice**

Combine the apple cider, cloves, allspice, cinnamon sticks, orange juice, and lemon juice in a large pot. Bring to a boil over medium-high heat. Reduce the heat to low, and simmer for 10 minutes. Strain and serve hot, or put in containers and chill for transport. Reheat before serving. Serve in mugs with cinnamon sticks.

For a cocktail version: Add a shot of Fireball Whiskey or any whiskey you prefer and a sprinkle of ground cinnamon.

❯ **Makes 8 to 10 servings.**

# ACKNOWLEDGMENTS

## KIX BROOKS

It's hard to know where to start to give thanks on this book. It's really about a lifetime of growing up around people who made cooking so much a part of their lives. It's really not about the kitchen at all, but about getting together with people you love and having something to do besides small talk. A grill or smoker, a big pot of water or oil, can all lead to a fun time together. My grandfather, father, and aunts and uncles all showed me both sides of how much fun cooking can be. Gathering with friends and family is half of it, and before you know it, there's a meal coming together. So I guess what I'm trying to say is: thanks to all my friends and family who ever had a garden, or took me fishing or hunting, or on a trip to Morgan City to get fresh oysters, or stopped at a roadside stand for fresh shrimp or peaches or tomatoes or whatever. Thanks to all my peeps who took the time to actually send recipes that I have loved over the years. Beyond all this culture that I was blessed with, thanks to Donna Britt for caring enough to stay on me and make sure this was more than an idea, for getting these great photos taken, and for organizing what would have most likely been a bunch of chaos without her—that would have never seen the light of day! It's a book I'm going to go look at again and again before I decide what's for dinner!

# DONNA BRITT

Thanks to my dear friend Kix for trusting me to help him with this book and for sharing his stories and recipes. Thanks to Barbara Brooks for digging out recipes, printing and scanning, following up on loose ends, and making sure Kix and I had our facts straight! As the saying goes, "It takes a village," and we had the best village possible bringing this book together! I would especially like to thank Tambi Lane for her beautiful photography, Caitlin Kelly for her great eye, and James Lewis for his culinary prowess, spot-on taste buds, and unending support. Thanks as well to John (J. P.) Kelly for inspiration, Patsy Britt for sharing, and the rest of my family (Donnie, Jamie, Jenn, Desi, Devyn, Tina, Sarah, Luke, Joy, and John L.) for putting up with me while I was obsessed with writing and cooking and finding the right plates, pots, and forks! Thanks to my friends who lent their hands and their pie pans and their time to help on this project: the Reynolds family (Kim, Rik, and Jak), the Mason family (Paula, John, Ruby, and Jack), Linda Lou and Shanda, and to my Granny Agnes who was the one who got me into the kitchen in the first place and who was watching over me every step of the way. A big thank you to Wendie Every and her creative team at Every Idea, as well as Matt at Mojo Rain. And finally, a huge thanks to Kix's crew at Maverick, including Clarence Spalding, Marne McLyman, Amanda Cates, and Madalyn Hankins, and to all the fine folks at HarperCollins/Thomas Nelson Publishing who have brought this book to life.